FABULOUS FEMALE MUSICIANS

SAMMY STEIN

CONTENTS

FOREWORD

by Vick Bain

As someone who has spent the past four years solely focused on researching and campaigning on behalf of women in music, and over a quarter-century working in the UK music industry, I am vividly aware the written canon about musicians is unquestionably male-dominated. A cursory look at a bookshelf on the history of music or musicians, songwriters, and composers, paints a picture of women being almost entirely absent from this important cultural art form. Except we are questioning that presumption now; women were always there; they just weren't necessarily deemed worthy to be written about. Therefore, it is of great importance that women are written into the record, and I welcome Sammy's wonderful contribution to this growing body of knowledge.

I became aware of Sammy in the summer of 2020. Most of us were at that stage living in an entirely online world, creating new connections virtually, and I was thus contacted by Sammy via my website regarding any facts and figures I may have had regarding women in jazz for her excellent book *Gender Disparity in UK Jazz*. I soon learned that Sammy's credentials as a fan, curator, researcher, and writer of all things jazz speak for themselves. She has written for premier platforms and publications and hosted numerous radio shows, and among various accolades has won a *Jazz Times* Distaff Award, the *Phace* Magazine's Music Book of The Year award, and she has her writing in the Library of Congress. Learning about this, I agreed to extract and send her jazz-specific data I had gathered for my report "Counting the Music Industry," what I termed a "gender gap audit" of UK music publishing and record label rosters to ascertain participation, and economic investment in, women musicians across all genres. It was clear there were cultural issues across the music industry but particular nuances within the jazz community, and Sammy systematically outlined much evidence to explain the reasons for these statistics and how we can change them for the better.

Sammy also excels in collections of interviews, as evidenced in her previous books *Women in Jazz* (8th House Publishing) and *In Their Own Words: Interviews with Women in Jazz*, (8th House Publishing), and so she returns to this approach in this new collection: *Fabulous Female Musicians*. This is her fifth book on music, and gives personal, first-testimony accounts of some of the issues raised in gender disparity in interviews with twenty-one women, most of whom are hugely successful in their own music genres and instruments, winners of Grammys and other prestigious awards. Sammy's standing and reputation in music has enabled her to reach out to these women across the globe, and her insightful questions illicit illuminating responses.

There are a number of interesting themes resonant, including the reflection that things are getting better for many women in music. The optimism in these pages is positively infectious and undeniable. Also strongly evident is their shared love and passion for music, shining out through all of their words, acting as a lodestone in their lives; they "were born to be musicians." However, mirroring my own research, some do still recount descriptions of having experienced overt sexism, bullying, and racism. Others are steadfast in their determination to have ignored it. Either way, all have developed "thick skins" and other coping mechanisms. No musician wants to be known more for their gender than their music and this frustration is voiced numerous times in these accounts; to be told "you play great for a girl" or to be welcomed at a professional gig as "the pretty lady" is a patriarchal view of the world that all of these musicians wish to be consigned to the past.

Therefore, *Fabulous Female Musicians* is a compelling read for anyone interested in what it takes to succeed in music (and indeed some explore what do we mean by success?), especially as a female musician. The testimonies these women have provided form a readable, powerful, and inspirational collection. Thus, Sammy has ensured that the names of these women will become part of the oeuvre of books about musicians in the early part of the twenty-first century.

INTRODUCTION

Music speaks to us on different levels. It can help create an atmosphere in films, set the mood in adverts, accompany games, and you can have it on as background or immerse yourself in a live concert. Music unites people and can alter our outlook.

Women have been part of music's evolution, but historically those who composed, performed, recorded, presented, and wrote about music were mostly men. Men, in effect, controlled music in all its forms.

However, for decades a quiet revolution has been happening— the rise of the female musician and the increase of her power.

With changing social, political, and moral attitudes, women are finally seen as equal to men. They no longer need to prove themselves or outshine men time and time again. They are a welcome and enriching presence in music. While society continues to develop a more egalitarian attitude, women take places once occupied by men, from bandleaders to soloists, producers to lecturers and professors of music. Gradually, we are seeing changes in attitude and an acceptance of everyone as equal, merited for their talent. Or are we?

What does being a female musician today really look like? Is it a myth to believe we are at that place where we can say all is equal in music?

To find the truth, I interviewed twenty-one female musicians who are at the top of their profession. Many are exemplars of how being female is no obstacle to success. They play many genres, from folk, jazz, classical, popular, blues, soul, and ragga. They are from different countries—India, Azerbaijan, the UK, Asia, America, and more. Some began their musical journey as a child while others began it later in life. All are working professionals, with different viewpoints and advice. Though many were drawn from the jazz field, their musical interests and success span many genres.

I asked each woman how they came to music and found the instrument they specialize in. I asked each woman a similar set of questions about their music career, so I could obtain comparisons. I asked them about their journey, whether they had experienced discrimination or bullying, and how they might advise female musicians wanting to make a career in music.

The answers varied, but the passion these professionals feel for music is palpable. I believe the answers offer revealing insights into the life of a female musician.

This book is about what music means to these female musicians, their influences, and the drive that fuels their passion. Apart from edits for grammar, the interviews are the women's own words.

As female musicians are acknowledged and step forward, what is clear is that the presence and success of female musicians enrich music beyond what we ever thought possible. I am grateful that so many busy, dedicated, and outstandingly talented female musicians were willing to be interviewed and share their journeys.

ELLEN ROWE

Photo Credit: Peter Smith

"The future is very rosy for female musicians—we are being taken increasingly seriously as awareness grows and some of the older possibly misogynistic generations fade out of the picture a bit."

Ellen Rowe is a jazz pianist, composer, and the Arthur F. Thurnau Professor of Jazz and Contemporary Improvisation at the University of Michigan. Ellen has won many coveted awards and performed across the US, as well as in Europe, South Africa, and Australia. She is an active clinician and has given masterclasses and workshops in many places. As a guest artist, she has enhanced the stages of many festivals and other events, including radio shows. Acknowledged as an outstanding compose, her compositions and arrangements have been performed around the globe. Her accolades are impressive, and she is a much-respected musician. Ellen is active within the Jazz Education Network and is on the board of the International Society of Jazz Arrangers and Composers.

SS: Can you tell me how you came to play music and how you found the instrument you specialize in? Do you play other instruments?

ER: I grew up in a very musical household (both parents went to Juilliard), and I inherited perfect pitch from my dad. There were two pianos in our living room, and it was natural for me to head over and try to play melodies back from records our family would listen to. I think I started doing that around age three. I also played flute pretty seriously from third grade up, though I had to back off on it when I went to college. I also taught myself bassoon in high school!

SS: What genres do you play?

ER: Jazz is my first love, though I also did a lot of classical accompanying while I was in college. I listened to a lot of Joni Mitchell, Carole King, Elton John, Crosby, Stills & Nash while I was growing up. In college, I discovered Earth, Wind & Fire, Tower of Power, and other funky horn bands. There is usually more stress surrounding any classical playing I do (which isn't very much these days), but all the other styles I mentioned fill me with great joy.

SS: Have you ever felt treated differently as a female musician? If so, can you tell me how and whether you were able to do anything about this?

ER: I have been treated differently all my life, though nowadays it is much better, now that I am an established artist and pedagogue. I felt overlooked as a pianist in college because I didn't have a McCoy (Tyner), Chick (Corea), or Oscar Peterson type of technique—I was told I sounded "too much like Bill Evans," which is actually a huge compliment, though it wasn't meant that way. As I started my college teaching career (I was twenty-four at the time), I found it hard to be very confident and often would have older men telling me how I should dress, approach my classes, set up my jazz ensemble, etc. That started to wane once they realized I knew what I was doing. I learned to politely say I had my own way of doing things that worked well, but I appreciated their offer to help. While I was in college, I would get hit on by older players on the club dates I would do, which was very hard to deal with as I wanted to get rehired. I learned to say that I had a boyfriend who would be very upset if anything happened to me. Things have improved drastically over the years, fortunately, thanks to greater awareness of power imbalances and "codes of conduct." I teach my female students to think ahead and have responses ready so that they don't get taken by surprise.

SS: Have you ever been bullied in your career as a musician?

ER: I have occasionally been told I was responsible for the music not going well (tempo slowing down, changes not being outlined, etc.) when in fact it was my male colleagues who were the problem. In those situations, I learned to not say anything back but to chat with my fellow rhythm section players to brainstorm how "we" could make the music better.

SS: What experiences in music have made you grow as a musician? Were there events that had a profound effect on you?

ER: Pretty much any experience that has pushed me outside my comfort zone either as a player or as a bandleader. Leading a few gigs with a quintet of Kenny Wheeler, Don Thompson, Pat, and Joe LaBarbera forced me to step up my game. Playing the Stravinsky piano concerto did the same. From an emotional standpoint, transformational experiences include getting to play Maria Schneider's music with her conducting and getting to perform Kenny Wheeler's "Sweet Time Suite" with him playing. More recently, presenting trio "edutainment concerts" that have called on me to transcribe and perform music by Barry Harris, Oscar Peterson, Bill Evans, and Mary Lou Williams have also been inspiring and transformational.

SS: Who inspires you?

ER: My latest *Momentum* album is dedicated to women heroes of mine. Each piece was written as a tribute to important women in my life, including Dian Fossey and Jane Goodall, Geri Allen and Mary Lou Williams, Michelle Obama, unsung heroines of the Civil Rights Movement, my mother, long-distance running legends Joan Benoit Samuelson and Gunhilde Swanson and tennis and equal rights stars Martina Navratilova and Billie Jean King. All these women display qualities that are important to me—tenacity, courage, fighting for justice, grace, and dignity.

SS: What would you say music did for you?

ER: Music allows me to express myself and actually "discover" myself in many ways.

SS: Could music ever be just a job?

ER: When I used to play all kinds of different music to pay the rent, it definitely could become a job, but nowadays I am privileged to get to pick and choose the kinds of gigs and concerts I want to take.

SS: What would you say to an aspiring female musician? Would you recommend music as a way to make a living?
ER: It is possible to make a decent living and I would highly recommend a career in music, but in addition to being a great player, you also need to believe in yourself, learn how to handle yourself on gigs where you may be the only woman, and be extremely professional in all your dealings and gig preparation. In many ways, the expectations are lower, so I like to surprise the hell out of people and set the bar as high as possible.

SS: If you had to explain the one thing that makes music worthwhile, what would this be?
ER: The chance to communicate with other musicians on such a deep level. Improvisation requires a high level of sensitivity and interaction, and when everyone is engaged deeply in that, it is one of the best feelings in the world.

SS: Do you think the pandemic changed music and how we access it? Or do you think music and how we access it changes over time in any case?
ER: I'm sure it changes over time with technological advancements, but the pandemic showed us how important music was to begin with, as so many musicians went to extraordinary lengths to continue to share their art. I think more people learned to consume shows digitally, which is both a good and bad thing.

SS: Thinking of that young aspiring musician, how would you advise her and what might her strengths need to be?
ER: Versatility helps, as does a willingness to teach privately (or possibly in a school situation) and to have skills as an arranger, composer, copyist, producer, sound engineer, etc. Being a savvy businessperson with a good sense of how to publicize gigs and do PR is very important. If you are lucky enough to be able to hire someone to help you, all the better!

SS: How do you see the future for female musicians?
ER: The future is very rosy for female musicians—we are being taken increasingly seriously as awareness grows and some of the older possibly misogynistic generations fade out of the picture a bit. There are all kinds of great women jazz players, young and old, who are playing as side people or leading their

own groups. More women are being hired in pro big bands (finally!) as well as directors of All-State Honor High School groups, and there is more of an awareness to play music written by female-identifying composers.

LENI STERN

Photo Credit: Sandrine Lee

"I see the future of music as bright and wonderful. It's one of the greatest gifts we have, and things are getting easier for women."

Leni Stern is a gifted guitar player, composer, and producer. She has inspired many with her playing and is defiantly a female bandleader, composer, producer, and proud of it. A five-time winner of the prestigious Gibson's Female Jazz Guitarist of the Year award, this Munich-bred New Yorker continues to produce astounding music. Her music has received stellar reviews in major publications. She produced an album, Dance, *during the pandemic, but another earlier one,* Smoke, No Fire *was produced in Mali during a military coup, so Leni is used to finding ways to create music even if conditions are not ideal. As well as playing guitar, Leni plays the n'goni—the "rhythm harp" of West Africa. Her marriage to fellow guitarist Mike Stern has led to the exploration and integration of styles, from blues and rock to jazz. Leni was a student of the mighty Bill Frisell at the Berklee College of Music in Boston and has performed with him and drummer Paul Motion. Her collaborators have included David Sanborn, Bob Berg, Wayne Krantz, Frisell, John McLaughlin, Michael Brecker,*

Esperanza Spalding, Brian Blade, and countless others. Recently, travels to West Africa have influenced her music, and the rhythm and legato potential of the guitar has been further explored. Her collaborations with Bassekou Kouyate and Ami Sacko have yielded new directions and possibilities for this ever-evolving musician.

SS: Can you tell me how you came to play music and how you found the instrument you specialize in? Do you play other instruments?
LS: I found my mother's guitar as a child and taught myself. When my mother noticed that I preferred the guitar to the piano, she sent me to her guitar teacher. I also play percussion and the n'goni, an African instrument.

SS: What genres do you play? Do you have a favorite?
LS: I play jazz, African music, funk, and blues. The guitar works well in many styles. I really like African music and the African way of playing the electric guitar.

SS: As a female, have you ever felt treated differently as a musician than if you were male? If so, can you tell me how and whether you were able to do anything about this?
LS: Of course, you get treated differently as a woman. The electric guitar is still viewed widely as a male instrument. Things changed when *Purple Rain* came out and Prince's band had two women in it, Wendy and Lisa. I got a call for a job the day after the movie was released, and then Michael Jackson had Jennifer Batten. Slowly, bandleaders started to think that it was cool to have a woman in the band on electric guitar. However, to this day I get comments from the audience that sound very surprised about what I do. It has not become normal yet and it is difficult. It is very tiring to constantly have to prove yourself. I feel that all I can do is be an example and show how much fun it is.

SS: Have you ever been bullied in your career as a musician?
LS: I have been studying martial arts, Hung Ga, and kung fu for twenty-five years. No, I don't get bullied. I highly recommend it. It is great to not feel physically threatened and to worry instead if you might get arrested for assault if your anger gets the better of you.

SS: *What experiences in music have made you grow as a musician? Were there events that happened that had a profound effect on you?*

LS: I think what made me grow most as a musician is playing with great players. I was very fortunate to play with Paul Motion and Bill Frisell early on. I recorded my first two records with them. I was terrified, but I made it through, and I came out a different guitar player. Playing with Salif Keita and Baba Mal had a profound effect on my music. It's hard to tell sometimes how it happens but you realize sometime later that you're not the same anymore. Or sometimes you don't realize at all and people tell you.

SS: *Who inspires you and why?*

LS: My husband, Mike (a well-known guitar player, played with Blood, Sweat & Tears, Miles Davis, and many more), is my main inspiration. Then there are all the great bebop players: John Coltrane, Miles Davis, and Wayne Shorter. I also listen to a lot of classical music, which, since I was born in Europe, is where I come from, but I also get inspired by visual arts, by nature.

SS: *What would you say to an aspiring female musician? Would you recommend music as a way to make a living? What characteristics do you need?*

LS: Music has been very good to me. Of course, I would recommend it to anyone. It's not easy, but nothing fabulous is! You just have to love music a whole lot to make it work!

SS: *If you had to explain the one thing you found that makes music worthwhile, what would this be?*

LS: I believe being a musician is a calling. The best way I can try to explain it is that you feel you have to do it, you won't be happy if you don't, and nothing else thrills you quite the same way.

One of the great things about being an improvising musician is that you can communicate with people all over the world, even if you don't speak their language. And you can communicate with other musicians in a very deep, intimate, and fun way. There's nothing quite like it. Maybe dancing?

SS: *Do you think the pandemic changed music and how we access it? Or do you think music and how we access it changes over time in any case?*

LS: Of course, music changes, everything changes, always. On the technical level, it is much easier to access music now.

The pandemic was a blessing and a curse for musicians. We lost all our jobs, but we got to practice for a long time and now everybody's coming out of the gate burning.

SS: Thinking of that young aspiring musician earlier, how would you advise her and what might her strengths need to be?
LS: It is definitely possible to make a good living as a musician. But you need to be proactive. You can't just sit at home and wait to be discovered. Music is a community, and you need to be active in that community. Go to all your friends' shows and bring people. Follow other musicians online, contribute to their efforts, and go to hear music any chance you get! Be the friend you wish you had!

SS: How do you see the future of music for female musicians?
LS: I see the future of music as bright and wonderful. It's one of the greatest gifts we have, and things are getting easier for women all around. Music is no different. I am very encouraged when I see young players come up and being confident and sounding great.

CHINA MOSES

Photo Credit: Sylvain Norget

"We are not all going to win. We are not all going to succeed, and for that one artist who is 'making it' whatever that resembles for you, there are millions that have tried."

China Moses straddles many genres from hip hop to blues and delivers powerful vocals with grace and commitment. She has recorded several albums and appeared on TV many times. She presents radio shows and playlists and is a voice-over artist. She has established a huge fanbase both in Europe and the US and continues to evolve vocally and shows no sign of staying in any kind of box where she can be labeled. I have worked with China before when she offered me material for my previous books, and she is as interesting and mercurial in person as her music.

SS: Can you tell me how you came to play music and how you found your instrument?

CM: I was born into an artistic family. Music has always been around me. I started doing music as a way to translate my emotions. I had trouble speaking about my emotions as a child. My father (the pioneering director Gilbert Moses) was sick with cancer, and I loved him dearly and I found that through music I could cope better. My mom (Dee Dee Bridgewater) found taking me to a child therapist didn't go too well. So, I started singing. Voice is my instrument; it is my only instrument and my first instrument. I play hyper basic guitar and piano, but yes, I found my voice through dealing with pain and facing death as a small child around ten or eleven years old.

SS: What genres do you play? Do you have a favorite genre?

CM: For me, music is music. As Duke Ellington said, there is no good or bad music. I make Black American music because that is my culture and heritage as a Black American. Music can differ in tempo, intensity, volume, the number of instruments and speed of the main melody and everything, but it all makes me resonate and gives me the ability to resonate with others, and so all Black American music is my favorite "genre"—and that makes it a pretty wide spectrum, from blues to hip hop, funk, soul, folk rock, Americana, jazz—it's all within me, and it is all my music and all of my heritage as a Black American.

SS: As a female, have you ever felt treated differently as a musician than if you were male? If so, can you tell me how this made you feel and whether you were able to do anything about this?

CM: Of course, as a self-identifying woman, I have been treated differently. I have been belittled, I have been ignored, I have been objectified—I have been so many things. I try to do something about it every single time. If I feel it is happening, I do try to speak out, try to have the conversation, and I do have to sometimes, as they say, "put my foot down" and then that gets you the reputation for being a diva, but you know what, I would rather be a diva than a pushover, so...

I think a lot of self-identifying women in music still have a lot of trouble with this debate, even though it has changed and gotten better, but I still think we have a long way to go. The only thing I can do is voice when I feel as if something is happening to me because I am Black, I am a woman, or I am a singer. There are so many different levels, and it is a very delicate tightrope walk to walk around earth as a Black woman within the realm of jazz, which is dominated by white male promoters.

SS: Have you ever been bullied in your career as a musician? If so, can you explain this and how it made you feel?
CM: Well, my life is my career and I have always been bullied. But at the same time, the bully is not here and I am. How does it make me feel? It makes me feel like shit, but then you lick your wounds, and you keep on going.

SS: What experiences in music have made you grow as a musician? Were there events that happened that had a profound effect on you?
CM: There are events every year that have a profound effect on my vocal evolution. And there are so many experiences I have had. One experience was going over to see Archie Shepp at his house in the suburbs of Paris with his wife Monette and my godmother Fara C, and Archie opened up the door and he was listening to some songs from my album *Nightintales,* and he was reciting back my lyrics and told me I needed to keep on writing and composing and my father would have been proud. Other moments include eating breakfast in a very fancy Japanese hotel and having Benny Golson come up and just tell me, "You'd better keep on doing what you're doing cos you sound good." It's getting a Facebook message from Ahmad Jamal saying that he believes in me. It's getting an email from Patrice Rushen saying she likes my music and that she is proud of me.

It's the moment where I sing off-key. It's the moments where I missed coming back in from a solo coming to the bridge. There are so many moments, and I have been doing music professionally since I was sixteen, so there are way too many moments to focus on one. Hearing yourself for the first time on loudspeakers in the studio, well that definitely affected me when I finally heard my voice.

SS: Who inspires you?
CM: Everyone inspires me. But I am primarily inspired by artists, musicians, and people who live their life out loud and free. From James Baldwin to Nina Simone, to Queen Latifah and Janet Jackson. Meshell Ndegeocello, Tori Amos, Bonnie Raitt, Frida Kahlo, Millie Jackson, Dinah Washington. I am inspired by all the artists that surround me and all the art that I have gotten to witness in my life. Georgia O'Keeffe, Matisse, and Bisa Butler. I am just inspired by art on a daily basis. I am inspired by the beauty that humans have to create art no

matter the circumstance, whether it is war or excruciating human existence. Art is always creative, and that inspires me.

SS: If you had to explain, what would you say music did for you? Could it ever be just a job?
CM: Music is a job. Performing is a job. But it is also my art and something that I can do. I can't imagine not doing it. Music is my life. Music kept me alive, and if I did not have music, I wouldn't be here probably. But sometimes you do "phone it in," sometimes you're elsewhere on stage, you know? But don't get it twisted. If you are a full-time musician, that is a job, and sometimes it can be just a job, depending on where you are in your life—but music is my livelihood.

SS: What would you say to an aspiring female musician? Would you recommend music as a way to make a living? What characteristics do you need?
CM: If you are looking for financial security, the way of the arts is definitely not the way to go, period. You need drive, you need to be able to communicate with others, you need to be able to listen, to apply yourself, you need discipline, you need so many things. I think being a full-time artist and paying your rent with your art necessitates you not ever giving up. So, would I recommend music as a way of making a living? Not if you want financial stability, but you can make a living doing music and you also *may* make a living doing music, but it may not be the music you want. There are so many ways to "do music" and be part of the larger music world. So, of course, I would say to any aspiring self-identifying female, "Come on, let's go!" It is a tough job. You may have to have multiple jobs, but if it is something you can't do without, why would I discourage you?

SS: If you had to explain the one thing (or more) you found that makes music worthwhile, what would this be?
CM: That's a very good question. Communion is what makes music worthwhile for me. And then also the joy. Also, the platform to express our inner, deeper emotions that cannot come out with words. Do you know what? It's all worthwhile.

SS: Do you think the pandemic changed music and how we access it? Or do you think music and how we access it changes over time in any case?
CM: Both of those are true. Music does change over time. In any case, how we access it changes over time because of technology, and because of the

formats music is distributed on. The pandemic changed things because concerts stopped so people started putting out more studio stuff or going through their archives, releasing live albums, and the radio shows and streaming platforms became our go-to place to hear something so necessary for most people in this world. There are few people I have met who say they don't like music, and I tend to avoid people who say they do not like music, you know? That is where I draw the line. I am not saying I don't like them, but if someone says, "I am not really into music," we have no connection. And that's all right; that is okay with me.

SS: Thinking of that young aspiring musician we imagined earlier, do you think it is possible to make a decent living as a musician? How would you advise her to do this and what might her strengths need to be?
CM: It depends; it really, really depends. Listen, if you are trying to get into music to make a living, give up music. If that is what you are being led by, stop right there. Or go and work on a cruise ship. The music industry is not for the faint of heart, and if you are trying to run after the bag (as in money bag), go ahead, but a lot—a lot—fail. There is one thing that people don't talk about enough—they don't talk about the chance factor. We are not all going to win. We are not all going to succeed, and for that one artist who is "making it," whatever that resembles for you, there are millions that have tried. That is why I do not take it lightly that almost thirty years into professionally making music, I am still working and performing. You can have a good manager if you are lucky. I have never had a manager and am just starting to work with a manager now.

You do need to be a businessperson. You need to take care of all things— there are a lot of things we need to take care of as an independent artist nowadays. There is a lot of back work that goes on, but there are as many different stories as there are artists, so all I can say is that I have been very lucky. I have also acknowledged everyone who has helped me along the way. I uphold them all in high regard, and for me what makes the difference between aspiring, struggling and success is making good music, having good taste, and sometimes that can't be taught. But some people find a formula and run with it. Some people make one hit. Some people never have any hits but live a long life in music. I don't know. The difference is years on the job, practice, determination, and devotion.

SS: How do you see the future for music? How do you see it for female musicians?

CM: Of course, many positive changes, come on. Anyone who says differently is blind. We have a long way to go though. But there are many positive changes. The future of music? I don't know, I don't have a crystal ball. All I can do is imagine a year ahead because that is how my concerts get booked, but day by day, right now, I think the future of music will be perfectly fine.

If it keeps on going how it is going now, there will be more and more women, it will be more and more equitable. I mean, it is free to do music anyway. We have fewer and fewer gatekeepers—and that is another conversation, but yeah, it is positive, all the changes are positive.

AMINA FIGAROVA

Photo Credit: Emmanuel Mohlame

"Music has always been there and will never die, and our paths as musicians, if you feel like this is all you live for, then it is all worth it... In music, probably more importantly than with some other professions, you have got to be absolutely crazy about what you are doing. You can't be afraid to sacrifice if you need to... If I had to explain one thing that makes music worthwhile, I would say, to me, music is like water. It is my life, what I was born to do. I do not know life without music or what it would be like."

Pianist and composer Amina Figarova is from Azerbaijan. She began composing when she was six years old. In Baku, Amina attended the Baku Academy of Music, studying classical piano. In 1988, at the Moscow Jazz Festival, she was invited to study at the Codarts University for the Arts in Rotterdam, where she developed her passion for jazz, and she completed her education in jazz performance at the Berklee College of Music in Boston.

Amina became involved with the Thelonious Monk Jazz Colony in Aspen, Colorado, and performed in jazz concerts with flutist Bart Platteau (who became her husband). Her compositions and accolades are many and her work has been praised by many writers. DownBeat *named her as a Rising Star Composer in 2014 and 2015.*

Amina performs with her group at prestigious venues in Israel, Europe, United Arab Emirates, Mexico, the USA, Azerbaijan, and many other countries. She has also performed at festivals and other events with her septet and the Amina Figarova International Quintet.

SS: Can you tell me how you came to play music and how you found the instrument you specialize in? Do you play other instruments?
AF: I started early. I was born into a very musical, non-musician family. Almost my entire family work in medicine, but I believe my grandmother played seven instruments. My mother played a little; my uncles and everyone was musical in my family. We had a piano in our house, and apparently, when I first touched the piano, my mother explained about keeping time, playing with one finger, and then I picked up melodies I heard on TV and radio. It felt like music found me, not that I found it—it was just there, and, according to my parents, when a record was on—they played a lot of jazz—I was trying to sing along with the records. Since then, it became an obsession. I did not care about toys or anything else. My toys became my audience. I was obsessed and played anything I could. My mother bought me a baby grand piano, and when I was about three, I composed a song, and ever since then, I started coming up with songs almost constantly. I was encouraged rather than pushed by my family. We were traditional and would have music evenings as a family. We would eat, talk, and drink, and then my uncle would play, my grandmother might sing, and I was immersed in that, and so grew up with music in our family. Growing up in the Soviet Union, I was surrounded by great classical music, and in Azerbaijan, by traditional music and music that was popular in my country at the time. It was based on jazz, and American jazz was popular. I grew up listening to Herbie Hancock, Chick Corea, and lots of Stevie Wonder, who is probably one of my favorite people in the world. I don't play other

instruments, just the piano. Composition has been my passion all my life, and there was never a moment of doubt, question, or even little thoughts about doing anything else. It was clear to me that was what I wanted to do, and there was a call from a very early age.

SS: What genres do you play—how do they differ/make you feel? Do you have a favorite genre?

AF: Growing up, I was playing everything I heard around me. When I was six years old, I went to a music school and studied classical music. At the time, in that very strict Russian classical environment, I was not encouraged to play other styles, but at home I was. I played a lot of things I heard on TV and grew up appreciating every type of music. Since I was very much into listening to jazz, soul, R&B, and fusion, that was the music I listened to a lot, as well as funk—they became my spectrum, from classical to, of course, today, when I predominantly play jazz. I practice classical music all the time to keep up my chops. My mother took me to theaters and the opera, so I grew up listening to all the genres surrounding me. I think if I stayed in one genre it could be very narrowing for someone like me. I love exploring and, well, when I was little, I would write in the style of whatever music I was playing at the time, whether that was Mozart or whoever. When I started studying with a great cello player, I wrote chamber music for my teacher. When I was a teenager, I wrote some pop music compositions that were arranged for a big band. When I was in the Netherlands later, I wrote a musical—it is not a typical musical, but it is a musical. So, it was whatever took me, because I appreciate and love all genres. I love funk, I love fusion, and I always feel that life is too short to explore everything you love. If I could, I might be a full-time funk player, or dedicated to keyboards, or Latin music, or classical, writing for a symphony orchestra. As a player and composer, I think it is important to try to explore as much as you can, but with me, it is not just a curiosity and interest, I have a love for many genres. It is to do with a love of percussion, because I grew up in a culture where we inherited a great percussion culture, so every genre and style that has a lot of percussion—Central American, Cuban, African, modern style, are all dear to my heart, so I cannot ever limit myself and say, "that's it."

Of course, with my band, we perform mostly jazz, but one of my albums was more of a reflection of a mix of fusion and funk, and I am working on other projects with other styles. I cannot pick one.

SS: As a female have you ever felt treated differently as a musician than if you were male?

AF: So, I know there is a lot of conversation about women and equality, and I know many women have a lot of issues, but if I can explain the way I grew up.

I grew up in Azerbaijan—one of the first countries where women were voting—I think even maybe before European women were voting, so I grew up never knowing inequality. I have never known inequality, whether racial or male/female and I did not grow up in such an atmosphere. I have no idea what it is about classical music in the US or Europe, but when I grew up in classical music, I never had any issues. In a symphony orchestra, the spread was probably fifty-fifty between male to female musicians.

Later, when I moved to the Netherlands and started playing jazz, there was never a moment where I felt treated differently. In fact, I was treated with a lot of respect. I had, in my band, male musicians always—I am not sure why, but the only way I choose them is how they play, and it is based on the level of musicianship and professionalism. I have always looked up to musicians who were more advanced than me because I feel it is more interesting to play with musicians who know more than I do. I always felt very respected and pretty soon I created my own band, so it has never been an issue for me. When I studied in Boston in 1992 as part of an exchange, I never felt any different relationships or attitudes toward me, although I had heard of some issues one musician had, but I did not understand what it was about. I was only there for a few months. Later, when I moved to the US, I heard more about issues that some female musicians, mainly instrumentalists, had, and we talked about this. I have always tried to share my experiences, and hope that maybe the strength I have from the way I grew up can help other musicians cope with it.

To me, how you should look at anyone professionally has to do with the quality of that person and should never be anything to do with gender, so I have to say it is not just growing up in a country where women voted. My grandmother was the director of a big institution, and my mother's friend was a minister of education, so I am used to women being a living force. So, if I think back on my experiences in the US, maybe, if I had been thinking about this issue, I might be wondering things like "Hey, why did this guy not ask me to play. Is it because I am a woman?" but I never experienced that, so never had those feelings. Luckily, I have never been hurt by any treatment that was not respectful. I think maybe my attitude helped me—it helped me to kind of give the right energy to other musicians. I cannot tell because I haven't been in this situation, but when I talk to some musicians who have had a problem (and obviously, I cannot tell you the names but they are well known), they always expressed to me that they wanted to talk to me more because I was giving them some strength, and I am very happy to help any woman who has issues with this from the way I know it. I would share my story, my experiences, and how I feel, and maybe if I can help, I would be absolutely happy, because I can also imagine that if women feel they are not appreciated, it can affect how they develop, which is shameful, because anyone should be able to develop their career as a musician how they want. If I can help anyone in any way, it would be an honor.

SS: What experiences in music have made you grow as a musician? What events had a profound effect?
AF: I think the main event was the way I grew up, being surrounded by music literally 24/7 and waking up with music—we always had music in the house, and I was always practicing and playing. I went to the Baku Academy of Music, which was known as a "special secondary music school for the most talented children." It was a combination of a European type of conservatory for children and a regular school, so there were music classes in the morning and evening. At night we would go to the theater, and my mother took me to concerts since I was very young. All of it inspired me. Music was always very emotional for me. Since I was very little, I felt that lots of different rhythms were almost like a heartbeat. I could feel them in my heart. I would dance the drum breaks and sing songs from the bottom of my heart because I felt emotional—it is hard to explain your emotional connection to music. It was not a case of seeking refuge in music because I grew up in a very loving and supportive family and we had lots of beautiful events. Lots of great live concerts that I've seen impressed me a lot. Of course, the records can too, but in live performances that I have seen—classical, operas, and jazz festivals (which were popular in Azerbaijan), I have been impressed by so many incredible musicians I can't even begin to think about how many. Whoever toured I would go and see if I could. I think it is a combination of lots of great musicians, so I cannot pick just one event, but the mass of constant musical influences meant I was feeling music all the time.

SS: Who inspires you?
AF: Inspiration is a very big word to me because it can come from anywhere, not just from your musical field. I have been inspired by my mother; although

she was not a musician, she was very musical. She was a psychologist and philosopher, and our daily conversations were like a trip to another planet. I loved philosophical conversations, and they made me think on another level since I was tiny. I loved analyzing feelings and events, because everything has a sound in my head and added some kind of musical layer. Just one example is many years ago I was in New York on September 11 (2001), and when I came back everyone was pretty traumatized because I had been pretty close, staying at a friend's house. When I came back to the Netherlands, I just wanted to take a break to recover from this traumatic experience, but then I saw a documentary and wrote a piece, and a second piece. Then my father passed away, so it became a tribute to mourning, and in a way, through the music I analyzed the emotion of mourning. After I wrote all the chapters of the piece, I spoke with my mother and we discussed reflections, analysis, and at that very deep analytical level she inspired me to analyze different events, whether they were happy or not. Whatever I see, not just major events but even if I see something happen on the street, it is always a multilayer in my head that parallels with music. And colors of course, because I have kinesthesia, so music and colors are very strong for me. So that is one of the main influences for me, besides many musicians I adore, like Ella Fitzgerald—my mother loved her, so I grew up hearing a lot of Ella and Joe Pass.

When I was in the Netherlands, I met Joe Pass when he came over for a masterclass, and that was amazing for me. I grew up also listening to a lot of Chick Corea and Herbie Hancock. I guess, just like everyone else, I had my own periods and times when I would just be listening deeply into this or that musician. Keith Jarrett has always been a true north in my life as well. He has been an influence. A great composer is Rachmaninoff. I played a lot of his music, and I am just amazed at the level of his creativity and harmony. Gil Evans and his project with Miles Davis too.

So, a lot of philosophy and psychology, from my mother, and writers like Dostoevsky, who write a lot of psychological books. So, between writers, actors, incredible musicians, and composers, I could go on for hours, but I don't think that is the idea here.

SS: What would you say music did for you? Could it ever be just a job?

AF: Music cannot ever be just a job to me. Even if I have to write a commercial tomorrow, it still cannot just be a job. It is my life; it is extremely emotional for me, and even if I... [Amina then paused while she reflected for a long moment before she continued]. You know it is interesting, because you might say, "Why do you care if you are writing music for, say, a lemonade commercial?" I have been in situations where I write for theater or other requests, but then I feel a bit like an actor (and I studied acting for a little while when I was younger). I understand that, you know, be that person, be that lemonade, be that whatever it is, and everything is very emotional to me—I mean everything *is* emotional, so if I have to write about that lemonade I can maybe become a child and think how I am that bottle of lemonade. It may sound silly, but to cut a long story short, it cannot be just a job for me. It is always emotional, and it always runs very deep—different layers and levels. And it is linked strongly with colors. I have been seeing colors since I was probably about six years old—that also triggers emotions, and it does not always translate in the bad or good but into maybe very fine emotions, but it always runs deep. Even if I hear music in the background, it always triggers something in me.

SS: What would you say to an aspiring female musician?
AF: The way I see the world is not about whether it is male or female, because you have got to be a great musician whether you are female or male. There is no other way. Is music a way to make a living? Absolutely, but anything can be a way to make a living. Literally anything, and in music, probably more importantly than with some other professions, you have got to be absolutely crazy about what you are doing. You can't be afraid to sacrifice if you need to. Or if you love it so much that you don't care about other things. You should not care about "Oh I can't do this or that, or plan events in my life, or not see my family or go to a party." I strongly believe, no matter what you do, if you are mad crazy about what you do and be madly in love with it, you will be successful and make money. I think to start your life saying "I will become a musician and make money" is very silly, because, as we all know, life in art is not easy, whether that is music, visual arts, ballet, or any other. Dedication and being really madly in love with what you do will bring success, through your qualifications—you will be qualified simply because you will practice, you will play, and do everything you can to get there because you can't do otherwise. Like you can't live without water, and if you can do, and if you do this, that will bring success and lead you to make money in what you do. A characteristic is determination and deep love and respect—you have to respect yourself and others and treat yourself the way you would treat others. As a musician, you want people to come and play your music, to come and play at a gig. You want

to play well, for them to hear you play every note, and you want all of that. If you want that, you have to do the same for others, so treat them as you would yourself. If I had to explain one thing that makes music worthwhile, I would say, to me, music is like water. It is my life, what I was born to do. I do not know life without music or what it would be like.

SS: If you had to explain the one thing that makes music worthwhile, what would this be?
AF: It is hard for me to find one or more things that make music worthwhile, but music is everything. Music is everywhere and born long before we were born. Birds are music, nature is music, and the sea and falling leaves are music. Music has always been there and will never die, and our paths as musicians, if you feel like this is all you live for, then it is all worth it. I hope I answered the question.

SS: Do you think the pandemic changed music and how we access it, or do you think music and how we access it changes over time in any case?
AF: The pandemic, the way I see it, arts and music survived a lot in our lives. If you think about it, over the centuries, the world has gone through wars, revolutions, the Industrial Revolution, and lots of dramatic events, and music and arts survived. They will never die, and musicians are key to this in our hearts; we know that and adapt to situations. If you read great poets—let's, say from around 1942–3—there was one great poet, Erich Fried, and he is just one example, he was a Jewish poet from Austria who had to escape to England. He adapted, he had to escape from the Nazis, but his art survived, and he wrote about it. That is just one example of how art survives, and we are the vessels that have to navigate through. The same with the pandemic. I think that events like those make us stronger. For many musicians, it was a difficult time and music was a refuge to find a way to express yourself—how the world feels and evolves around you. So, music describes events; it is almost like a history book, not just music but arts in general. I think it went along its natural path, in the same way as before. The same for listeners. The way we hear the music and the way we as listeners accepted it. I cannot be that objective as I am not just a listener, but I imagine the listeners could experience the view of the artists through what was happening, and it helped us come to healing and understanding. I think the pandemic is just one of many events that many artists have had to go through.

It is always good to have a plan, but flexibility is the most essential thing to have. Things might go differently for you than you planned, and if you are flexible things can go well. I think it is a combination of being well planned but also being flexible and intuitive. I think intuition is a very important aspect—at least it has been in my life. I think it has to do with risks. If you intuitively feel that taking a risk is worth it—depending on the situation, in general, I think it is of course discipline—planning your day well—if you do not do this you won't be practicing enough, but at the same time if you plan too much and become fixed on certain ideas, then you might be blind to other opportunities around you. It is like yin and yang, you need to have a combination of being well-organized, and great planning, but also be flexible and prepared for the unexpected. I am not sure if having a good manager is important or not. I have many friends around me who do have managers and there are lots who don't, and I don't think it necessarily reflects on their success. It might help in the beginning, but if you never take care of your business, you will never know how to do that, so it is important to be part of it.

SS: What makes the difference between aspiring, struggling, and being a success?
AF: The difference between being aspiring, struggling, and successful is that struggling is not really a main issue because almost everyone goes through times in their life when they may not have enough gigs, not make enough money, or have too many costs or whatever. This can happen at any point, not just when you are a beginner. It can happen later if you make certain decisions or investments, but I don't think that is a big issue. I think the most important thing, as I said before, is to be flexible. Don't get fixed on "I need *x* amount of dollars, or to play that place there." You might then make a wrong decision. As a musician, we are creative, so don't forget to keep creativity in every aspect of your life, even financially, because this is what it is to be an artist. I think that is probably what will help you to find your way to success.

SS: How do you see the future of music? How do you see it for female musicians?
AF: That is a huge question. The future of music? Well, as I said, music will never die, and that is for sure. The way it develops today, I think, maybe it is my hope, but I think there is always, no matter how much we get into creating using all the possibilities like digital instruments, loops, sound banks, and all

of that to do with technology, but it feels to me that there is always a relapse to acoustic instruments, to real instruments. I don't really worry that we will escape to a digital world and never play real instruments anymore—I know some people talk about that. I do not have a crystal ball, but I think genres will be widened and I think there will be even more of a mix between genres. Just as an example, when I was little in Azerbaijan, we had this great pianist and composer called Vagif Mustafazadeh, who played jazz and folk music from Azerbaijan—the folk music is based on improvisation and is called mugham. He used that in combination with traditional rhythms and fused this with jazz. This became hugely popular and is now known as mugham jazz, played by musicians including Rafig Babayev, Ibrahim Maalouf, and others. Others combine Indian music with jazz. This is just an example or two and simply has to do with people trying to bring genres together with their origins.

In the same way, one of our first composers in the twentieth century brought Azerbaijani traditional instruments into the symphony orchestra. We are not done with that and there will be more fusion and more interaction with other arts. I think this will happen more and more. I see positive changes, and from what I see, from my colleagues male and female, I feel there are lots of positive changes in the way people perceive music, their performance, and their interactions with each other. I think it is important to remember we are musicians. We consume music through listening. Maybe the audiences want to see you in a beautiful dress, but as musicians, we perceive music through listening. This is how we must perceive the music and listen to each other musically and verbally. Really listen, not necessarily look at who you are, just listen, whether my language, the way I speak musically, talks to you, no matter who I am, where I am from, if I am male or female—whatever. This is the most important factor—the way we hear the music is the only thing that matters. I think, if we continue doing that, we will be fine.

JAMIE BAUM

Photo Credit: Sandrine Lee

"Music is not just a job, it's a way of life, a way of being
and viewing the world."

*New York City-based flutist, composer, recording artist, producer, and clinician
Jamie Baum has toured globally and performed at major festivals and venues.
Her collaborations have included Randy Brecker, Roy Hargrove, Donald Brown,
Monika Herzig, Judi Silvano, Tom Harrell, Paul Motion, Kenny Barron, Jane
Bunnett, Anthony Braxton, Wadada Leo Smith, and many more.*

*She has been involved in projects, performances, and tours performing
classical, new music, Brazilian and Latin music and her list of awards and
grants is long and from varied origins.*

*Jamie has toured for the DOS/Kennedy Center Jazz Ambassador program in
South America and South Asia and has been sponsored by the State Department
on shorter tours. Her Septet has been together since 1999 and her other
projects include Short Stories Band, Yard Byard: The Jaki Byard Project, The
Richie Beirach/Jamie Baum Duo, and NYC Jazz Flutes.*

She has been on the faculty of the jazz department at Manhattan School of

Music since 2006, on the adjunct faculty roster at the New School University since 2004, and taught at Berklee College of Music.

SS: Can you tell me how you came to play music and how you found the instrument you specialize in? Do you play other instruments?

JB: I started playing the piano when I was very young, three years old, I think. My mother had gone to Juilliard pre-college and then for a year or two of college there before getting married, and had majored in piano and trombone. She taught piano lessons, though stopped teaching after she got married but started me on piano with a local teacher. I was very lucky because my parents took me to hear all sorts of music from a very young age (something most parents would not do), so I got to hear Louis Armstrong, Duke Ellington, Ella Fitzgerald, Dizzy Gillespie, etc., and a lot of classical music concerts (opera and symphonies). I took lessons until I was eleven or twelve years old but didn't practice much. Always classical until the last year when I studied jazz with pianist John Mohegan who lived a couple of towns away from me. I stopped playing piano pretty much after taking a year of those lessons until I took up the flute later in high school, though I was not very serious about it. It was fun to play an instrument that was more mobile than the piano, and I played it in the high school marching band for a year. I also took some lessons at that time with a sax/flute teacher at the local university who introduced me to various jazz recordings that had flute on them (i.e., Eric Dolphy, Rahsaan Roland Kirk, Hubert Laws, etc.). I still wasn't very serious about it though I did listen to a lot of different kinds of music and went to hear quite a bit of live music. In addition to jazz and classical, I liked rock (Jimi Hendrix, etc.) and "singer-songwriter" types like James Taylor, Joni Mitchell, Crosby, Stills, Nash & Young, and blues players like BB King and the Winter Brothers. It took me a long time to decide to become a musician, since it was something I really had never considered as a career path and had been focusing on other activities and had also been involved in some political activism while growing up.

When I finally went to the New England Conservatory of Music in Boston, I started there as a third-stream major and then after a year switched to the jazz program to focus more on learning the language and to play over changes. It was a wonderful school and I got to study with many great musicians including Jaki Byard, George Russell, Jimmy Guiffre, William Thomas McKinley, Ran Blake,

Joe Maneri, etc. I studied saxophone with Joe Allard for a year too but then decided to focus on the flute and composition since I didn't really have time to do all three. I still play piano well enough to compose but not well enough to do any gigs—and, of course, I play the flute, alto flute, flute d'amore, and bass flute. There were so many great musicians at NEC just before me and while I was there... so much creativity... and I met several long-lasting friends and colleagues whom I have continued to play with on and off over the years.

SS: What genres do you play—how do they differ/make you feel? Do you have a favorite genre and why?

JB: I have always enjoyed playing several different genres of music and never wanted to limit myself to just one. I have played and performed in jazz, classical, Brazilian, Latin, South Asian, and free/avant-garde type groups, though I'd probably say that I most often play in the modern jazz style. For me, it is more about the people I play with and not the genre. If the musicians are great, fun, and open to connecting, it can be an exciting and rewarding experience no matter the style... and it is always a challenge to try to understand the roots and characteristics of different styles. That's one thing I love about jazz; it is so porous and can incorporate so many influences. I think jazz has always been that way, and if you look at many of the important figures in jazz, they all looked to other styles at times for inspiration. Charlie Parker with strings, Dizzy Gillespie with Latin music, Stan Getz with Brazilian music, Coltrane was interested in South Asian music, Miles with rock and pop, etc.

SS: As a female, have you ever felt treated differently as a musician than if you were male? If so, can you tell me how and whether you were able to do anything about this?

JB: Well, when I first started, and for several years, things were very different for women in general, and it was unusual to be a female in the jazz field, and at my school (NEC), in fact, when I was there for my undergraduate degree, there were maybe three or four women instrumentalists in the jazz program the entire time. Of course, during those days, there were many times I was told by club owners, record labels, concert promoters, and agents that they wouldn't book a female bandleader because no one would come or be interested. I was also told so many times "You play great for a girl" and "You don't sound like a girl, you sound like a guy," and of course, that was meant to be a compliment. In terms of "what to do about it," well, my women musician friends and I just felt we had to work twice as hard to be accepted, and if we did, would hopefully get the opportunities at some point. Not having opportunities was probably the hardest part of it because it is difficult to improve and stay motivated if you don't get the opportunities to play and/or be part of the scene and various projects so as to be able to learn and grow. But things have changed a bit and you would most likely not hear anyone say those things now... I think it is different for the younger generation of women, though not a hundred percent of course. There are many great women players on the scene today who have many more opportunities than we did. It is much more acceptable to see women both as bandleaders and side women and taken for granted in many cases.

SS: Have you ever been bullied in your career as a musician, or come across bullying?
JB: I don't know if I would say I was bullied, but I was often made to feel like an outsider and not part of the scene, and not often included in the sessions or "hangs" musicians would have. Unfortunately, it made me feel that I always had to "prove" myself, that I was a serious musician, and prove I had studied and absorbed "the language." I think many musicians feel this way anyway, but it was particularly more acute for women. As I mentioned, things are quite different now in that regard.

SS: What experiences in music have made you grow as a musician? Were there events that happened which had a profound effect on you?
JB: It is difficult to answer this question briefly and specifically, since in one way or another all of my experiences have made me grow as a musician. I always learn something from each situation (if I am open to it), and can always find something to work on, get better at, and/or learn from, whether on a wedding gig (which I used to do in my early years), a jam session, or any gigs I'm on as a leader or side woman. That said, I've been lucky to have had so many opportunities to work with many great musicians, whether in my own bands, in other bands, or on tours and recordings I've done. One example... I had a few US State Department-sponsored tours to South America and South Asia where I had multiple opportunities to collaborate with top musicians in those countries, who are masters... whether watching them, playing with them, learning their music, or discussing music with them, the experience often had a profound effect on my musical direction or thinking.

SS: Who inspires you?

JB: Again, that can get lengthy, and my response can depend on my mood or the day you ask. It really started with my enchantment and obsession with Miles and Coltrane, and of course then the long lineage of iconic jazz musicians. I was always inspired by the way musicians like Miles, Wayne, Herbie, etc. would take risks and explore different styles of music and always evolve. Many of my peers whom I have been lucky to play with who are doing such creative things inspire me as well. My former teachers who continue to work hard and grow inspire me. Many women, both musicians and women in other fields (and my friends and former students) including those who have "paved the way" inspire me. I'm hesitant to name names for fear of leaving someone out! Of course, there are the friends and family members who faced serious illness and continued to fight and live their fullest, productive lives until the end who have inspired me... I think of them when things aren't going my way...

SS: If you had to say, what would you say music did for or to you? Is there some part it taps into? Does it make you feel emotional? Could it ever be just a job?

JB: I hate to sound clichéd, but music is not just a job; it's a way of life, a way of being and viewing the world. Especially as an improviser, it makes you more open and interested in what is going on around you, connecting with people and the environment you are in. It is an incredible commitment to be a musician, but I think the process of creativity and emotional and personal expression, when you can access that, is a very rewarding experience. At the very basic level, I think one has to enjoy, or at least find meaning and be committed to the process of daily, solitary practice, exploration, and (hopefully) growth, in addition to connecting with others through the collaborative experience of making music, because all of the other stuff that would constitute "success" (i.e., fame, fortune, etc.) is not guaranteed and can be elusive.

SS: Would you recommend music as a way to make a living? What characteristics do you need?

JB: Music, as a profession, requires a bit of sacrifice and is something you do because you can't imagine doing anything else that would "check all the boxes." I think I have explained some of my thoughts about this, but you do need perseverance, to feel comfortable spending time alone with your instrument, to be able to handle rejection, and be somewhat resilient.

SS: If you had to explain one thing that makes music worthwhile, what would this be?

JB: Well, I think what I explained before, but in addition, I love traveling and touring and find I enjoy the company of most musicians. I am a very curious person and music is an ongoing process of discovery and growth, and of course traveling and learning about other cultures and their music is very fulfilling in that way as well. There is also a great deal of satisfaction that comes from either/both accomplishing a challenge (i.e., some difficult music you weren't sure you could learn) and composing music that I'm happy with. It's a bit miraculous to create something out of nothing, whether that be a composition, an improvisation, or a piece of art, especially if others respond to it favorably or are moved by it.

SS: Do you think the pandemic changed music and how we access it? Or do you think music and how we access it changes over time in any case?

JB: I'm sure both are true. Everything affects music, but global seismic things like a pandemic, war or personal challenges like illness or the loss of a loved one can create major changes individually and/or collectively. Of course, with the pandemic, there were no live performances and many musicians turned to other ways to express or promote themselves, whether that meant composing, performing "online" live or pre-recorded, streaming, etc. And in some ways, those things that are affected by these external or internal shifts can be obvious immediately and others take time to reveal themselves or become apparent. In one case, it was interesting to see that those with knowledge, talent, and/ or comfort presenting themselves from home "online" seemed to be able to break through more readily, but again, it may take time to clearly see the effects and how things ultimately play out.

SS: Thinking of a young aspiring musician, do you think it is possible to make a decent living as a musician?

JB: At the time when I decided to devote myself to becoming a professional musician, things were very different in the music business for women and playing an instrument that was considered to be in the "miscellaneous" category. All of that has changed considerably, and of course "hindsight is twenty-twenty" as they say. On one level, to "jump in headfirst" into a field like "jazz," one might need to have an "unrealistic" or "fantasy" perception of their future, because knowing the reality would have probably prohibited them from doing so. Regarding making a "decent" living... well, that can be a bit subjective, in addition to several other factors, including where you live. For example, NYC is quite expensive and quite competitive because of the multitude of musicians. Making a "decent living" can also depend on a variety of other things (i.e., what instrument you play, style of music, personality type, etc.), but in general, it isn't easy.

SS: How would you advise her to do this and what might her strengths need to be?
JB: I think I might have thought more about taking up saxophone, practiced harder (though I did do that and still do)... maybe hang out and "schmooze" more, learn more of the business side of things, more of the technology side of things, etc.

SS: Does she need to be a businessperson, to plan, and get a good manager?
JB: Of course, all of that can't hurt! Seems quite helpful these days.

SS: What makes the difference between aspiring, struggling, and being a success?
JB: Again, that can be very subjective, and everyone has to decide what "success" means for them. Ultimately, again, there are so many factors that contribute to those things, including the very important "timing" (i.e., what you do is "in favor" with the press/audience/music world/biz at the right time), since there seems to be very little room at the top. It's a bit reflective of the way things are in society at this time—where a small percentage of artists get most of the festival bookings, tours visibility, etc., instead of things being spread out a little more evenly among the many deserving musicians.

SS: How do you see the future for music? How do you see it for female musicians? Have you noticed any positive changes—or not?
JB: It is difficult to project the "future for music," except for the fact that there will always be many people who will devote their lives to it. I never understand when people say "Nothing is happening in music these days," or "Jazz is dead." I disagree a hundred percent. I've been living in NYC for thirty years and there have always been exciting, creative, boundary-pushing musicians and interesting music being made... so I have no worries about that. The "music business" is a whole other thing, and it is difficult to say what will

happen. It's unfortunate, but with the whole "streaming" concept (Spotify, Apple Music, etc.) there is virtually no possibility for an artist to make any money from their recorded music, particularly jazz artists who don't usually sell or stream in the kinds of numbers that popular music does. The concept, respect, and importance of artistic and intellectual property rights seems to no longer exist, and it's difficult to predict where that will go and what sources of steady income will be available to most musicians other than from teaching. For female musicians, while there is still quite a way to go for parity, things are much better now than when I started, and overall, the stigma of being a female (or even the discomfort of being the only one) in a male-dominated field has diminished. In particular, I see many of my students not giving it a second thought.

MAGGIE NICOLS

Photo Credit: Self-portrait set up by Lily Bryant

"I feel I am a channel for divine, universal creativity, healing love, and liberation. I love how it [music] connects us all. It is meditation, it is free expression, it is a universal language."

Maggie Nicols has been involved in improvising music for decades and inspires fellow musicians to follow their dreams where music is concerned. Maggie's name gets mentioned a lot by musicians when discussing music's ongoing evolution. I recently found myself arriving too early for a gig and luckily the venue offered hot tea and a place to wait out of the cold in London's Dalston. Maggie came across and proved a warm and lively conversationalist. With platinum hair and a very striking bright red outfit, with "rebel" across the front, Maggie was undeniably present. Her music proved just as intriguing as her character, and she engaged the audience, especially when she involved them in a communal singing exercise. I still have vivid impressions of Maggie playing a keyboard and singing, completely lost in the music and that of the musicians she was on stage with. Maggie has been a dancer, musician, and singer and has worked with many improvisers in the UK, but she has also worked in Europe.

She joined The Spontaneous Music Ensemble in 1968 as a free improvisation vocalist and has been active in running workshops and involved in experimental theater. She was a member of the Keith Tippet's group Centipede and the Feminist Improvising Group and continues to forge relationships with different ensembles and work as a solo artist. When I asked her if she would be happy to be interviewed for this book, I was amazed and, quite frankly, delighted she said "yes" if she had time—and she made that time.

SS: Can you tell me how you came to play music and how you found the instrument you specialize in? Do you play other instruments?
MN: I play piano, but it has taken me a long time to trust that I deserve to play it. When I first came onto the jazz scene in 1963, I only saw men playing instruments and women singing. I assumed that women weren't capable of playing instruments! I think this is what motivated me to use my voice as an instrument. I also met a busker in Soho at the age of fifteen when I was working at the Windmill Theatre as a dancer, and he encouraged me to sing.

SS: What genres do you play—how do they differ/make you feel? Do you have a favorite genre and why?
MN: I started singing cabaret, soul, and blues and then fell in love with jazz and later free improvisation. I love all music. Soul touches me on a deep level, I love dancing to ska, and singing and playing free improvisation is truly liberating, nourishing, and inspiring, both individually and collectively.

SS: As a female, have you ever felt treated differently as a musician than if you were male? If so, can you tell me how and whether you were able to do anything about this?
MN: When I first started singing, I felt a lot of prejudice from some musicians who didn't like female singers, but my mentor, pianist Dennis Rose, always encouraged and honored me. Just keeping singing, whatever the obstacles, was what I did about it.

SS: Have you ever come across bullying or been bullied in your career as a musician? If so, can you explain this and how it made you feel?
MN: I was coerced and pressured into servicing some men sexually and that was disturbing.

SS: What experiences in music have made you grow as a musician? Were there events that happened which had a profound effect on you?

MN: Pretty much every experience both nourishing and abusive has played a part in making me the musician I am. I do not think that abuse is necessary for growth, however. Singing free improvisation with drummer John Stevens and saxophonist Trevor Watts in the Spontaneous Music Ensemble was life-transforming. Becoming a mother has probably been the most important thing in my life.

SS: Who inspires you?

MN: Musicians John Coltrane and Bill Evans for their ability to immerse themselves in the love of what they played. John (Stevens) and Trevor (Watts) for taking me safely into altered states through sound. Dennis for helping me sing bebop in meaningful soulful, authentic ways. My daughter Aura Vince because she is one of the gentlest, most creative souls I know. Pianist Irene Schweizer for her total integrity, inventiveness, and commitment to free improvisation. Anarchist Emma Goldman for her courage and dedication to social justice, free love, and the declaration that if she couldn't dance it was not her revolution. My mother Zouina Benhalla (an actress) who ran away from home to sing and act said, "to live is to create" or to "to create is to live." I can't remember which way around, but it works both ways. She refused to be defined by age, and her mantra was "J'aime la vie," I love life. She also used to talk in a made-up language with me when I was a child. My first experience of improvisation.

Everybody I sing and play with inspires me. Jeremy Corbyn for his gentle commitment to social justice in the face of slander and lies. Alice Walker for her profound compassion in her writing, alongside her committed activism. Dr. Cornel West for his dedication to truth-telling and his openness to communicating with those he disagrees with. There is not enough room here for all the people who inspire me. All those who dissent from the dominant narrative and risk exile.

SS: If you had to explain, what would you say music did for/to you? Is there some part it taps into? Does it make you feel emotional? Could it ever be just a job?

MN: It could never be just a job. It is my life's work. I suppose to express the essence, I feel I am a channel for divine, universal creativity, healing love, and liberation. I love how it connects us all. It is meditation, it is free expression, it is a universal language. As Mary Maria Parks sang, "Music is the Healing Force of the Universe."

SS: What would you say to an aspiring female musician? Would you recommend music as a way to make a living? What characteristics do you need?
MN: I would say, if you love it, do it, whether you make a living from it or not. If you can, find mentors, especially other women who exist now in ways that they didn't when I was a young singer. Find kindred spirits and never let yourself be pressured into doing something you don't want to do.

SS: If you had to explain the one thing (or more) you found which makes music worthwhile, what would this be?
MN: It brings love, connection, and inspiration in abundance.

SS: Do you think the pandemic changed music and how we access it? Or do you think music and how we access it changes over time in any case?
MN: For some of us, we went into ourselves and our creativity more deeply during lockdown, for others it was a traumatic experience of isolation and injustice. Music and how we access it is the same and not the same over time. As more women have emerged as strong role models, that has undoubtedly made access more welcoming and possible for young women coming into music. I think the dominance of formal music education though has also made it harder to learn by playing with more experienced musicians, which I found so helpful.

SS: Do you think it is possible to make a decent living as a musician?
MN: I can't speak very well on that subject. My living from music is precarious and yet I feel blessed to be paid, when I am, for doing what I love.

SS: How do you see the future for music? How do you see it for female musicians? Have you noticed any positive changes—or not?
MN: More women visible and playing has to be a positive thing. Music will always survive, as far as I can see, because sound is everywhere, and where there is sound, in birdsong, rivers, conversation, laughter, tears, etc., there is music and the inspiration for song composition, free improvisation, and a multitude of musical expression.

ZOE RAHMAN

Photo Credit: Ilze Kitzhoff

"I've been in a situation where I've asked a promoter at a club
if I could have a gig with my own band and been told,
'Give us a kiss and I'll think about it.'"

*Composer and pianist Zoe Rahman is from the UK and was brought up by
her Bengali father and Anglo-Irish mother in Chichester. She studied classical
piano at the Royal Academy of Music and gained a music degree at St Hugh's
College, University of Oxford. She won a scholarship to study jazz performance
at Berklee College of Music in Boston. She formed her trio with bassist Joshua
Davis and drummer Bob Moses. Zoe has been featured on radio and television
programs and performed for the BBC. She won Jazz Album of The Year at the
Parliamentary Jazz Awards in 2006 and in 2012 she won Best Jazz Act Award
at the MOBO Awards. I first saw Zoe when she was playing with Courtney
Pine, and was impressed by her talent and style. She has a way of completely
engaging an audience.*

SS: Can you tell me how you came to play music and how you found the instrument you specialize in? Do you play other instruments?
ZR: When I was about four, my parents bought an upright piano for ten pounds for my three siblings and me to play with. It had woodworm and candleholders and was bought more as a toy than an instrument. They noticed after a while though that we enjoyed playing it, so eventually my older sister went for lessons, and we all ended up learning. It was a very musical household. There was lots of music at school. We had a great primary school teacher who made music a part of everyday school life, teaching us recorders, guitar, and putting on musical shows. Outside school, I also learned flute, but the piano was always my main instrument. I went to the Royal Academy of Music from when I was eleven to eighteen every Saturday to learn classical piano and guitar.

SS: What genres do you play—how do they differ/make you feel? Do you have a favorite genre and why?
ZR: When I was a teenager, I went to a local jazz gig, and I was fascinated with how the music was being improvised and how the band interacted with each other as well as the audience. There was a great atmosphere, with a bar at the back where people could hang out. It was so different from the classical concerts I'd been to, and I immediately loved it.

I started to listen to jazz with my brother. We had albums by Miles Davis, Herbie Hancock, Ella Fitzgerald, and Nina Simone. We tried to play what we were hearing. The first solo I ever learned was Horace Silver's "Song for My Father."

I went to Oxford University to study music, but while I was there, I tried to get as much jazz playing experience as I could. I set up a jazz society as an excuse to invite guest artists to come and do gigs and give workshops and to go and see gigs, including traveling to London to go to Ronnie Scott's.

Jazz was my passion; I loved the sound of it, and I just wanted to learn to play it. I went to as many jazz gigs as I could, often just going on my own if I couldn't find anyone I knew who was interested! I wrote a dissertation on Bill Evans as part of my classical music degree and generally tried to shoehorn as much jazz into my life as possible. I'd go and talk to jazz musicians after their gigs, asking for advice and seeing if I could get lessons with them.

SS: As a female, have you ever felt treated differently as a musician than if you were male? If so, can you tell me how, and whether you were able to do anything about this?

ZR: It never occurred to me at all that there weren't many female musicians in the jazz world or that I might be treated differently because I was a woman playing jazz—it only dawned on me much later when I started to try and make a career out of playing jazz.

I remember going to a gig at the Jazz Café in London and I asked one of the musicians after the gig for advice on starting as a jazz musician. I told him I was a piano player. His advice was to think about singing as I'd make more money. It shocked me. I doubt he'd have said the same thing if a young man had asked him for advice.

On my first album, which I recorded in 2001, I decided not to put a photo of myself on the front cover, I just wanted people to hear my music and listen to what it sounded like, not judge it on what I looked like. When it was released, some tracks were played on the radio, which was exciting for me. A few weeks later, a musician, who also had released an album around the same time but who hadn't got any radio play, asked me how I got the music played on the show and asked, "Did you send in a photo?" He couldn't accept that the DJ had liked my music for what it was.

I'm treated differently as a woman on many levels, not just in music; it's a deeply rooted societal issue. Jazz has traditionally been a very male-dominated art form at every level—musicians, composers, radio DJs, magazine editors, promoters, sound engineers, photographers, record company bosses, educators, the list goes on. As a female jazz artist, it feels as if you're not really considered on an equal footing. There seems to be an assumption that you can't play, or you don't know what you're talking about unless you prove otherwise. Things are slowly changing now but those things still prevail.

SS: Have you ever come across bullying or been bullied in your career as a musician? If so, can you explain this and how it made you feel?

ZR: Jazz isn't the easiest career choice for anyone, so it's hard to compare with how other people have experienced the business, but all I can do is tell you the kind of comments and experiences I've come across. I've been told many times I "look like a singer." I've been told, as a compliment, "You play like a man," as if that's infinitely better than saying "You play like a woman!" I've been in a situation where I've asked a promoter at a club if I could have

a gig with my own band and been told "give us a kiss and I'll think about it."
At another club, when I questioned the low fee I was getting and asked if the
band could get paid more, I was told by the manager (in an attempt to be
helpful) that I could always come and waitress at the club if I was short of
money. I don't know if any of these things happen to male musicians. In the
lockdown of 2020, the only two live gigs I was involved with were offered to
me because the male musicians who were already booked had to cancel. The
only times my music has been published, I was recommended by a woman.

I know the industry has very much been based around the old boy's network,
I've just had to find a way around it. The audience I've built up a connection
with come to the gigs because they like the music; that's what has kept me
going. There's no replacement for the feeling you get when you perform
and can tap into people's emotions. I love the joy, the raw emotion, and the
creativity that jazz allows you to explore.

***SS: What experiences in music have made you grow as a musician? Were
there events that happened which had a profound effect on you?***
ZR: I've had some incredible support from many male colleagues over the
years, which has helped, but there are people in the industry who have turned
a blind eye (including women) when I've asked for help, so I've had to just
forge my own path.

I set up my record label in 2001 and I still put my albums out myself. I didn't
have a support network around me, so I took on most of the roles personally,
as many artists do—booking agent/tour manager/bandleader/composer/
record company boss/manager... I've asked over the years for help but very
little was forthcoming. I could see that many male artists around me (who had
won major awards or who'd put out successful albums like me), would get
agents or managers with ease. That never happened for me, despite many
years of asking!

It's been a hard journey, but I do it because I love the music. For my latest
album release, which is coming out in 2023, I decided I needed a team of
people around me—recording and touring an octet was too much work on my
own, particularly as I have two young children, so I've slowly managed to find
people to help me, the majority of whom, as it turns out, are women, including
my agent, publisher, photographers, videographer, live sound engineer, PR
team, some of the musicians and many of the promoters who've booked me.

SS: Who inspires you? Not just musicians, perhaps, but anyone, and can you explain how they inspire you and why?

ZR: I'm hugely inspired by anyone who devotes their life to playing music, and in particular, I'm inspired by female jazz musicians, especially composer pianists, as I know how hard it's been for me to write and produce my own music and to just get by in the industry. To be honest, I'm really tired of talking about being a woman in jazz, I just want to be a jazz musician. Can we please move on?!

SS: What would you say to an aspiring female musician?

ZR: Same as I'd say to anyone, do some practice!

SS: Would you recommend music as a way to make a living?

ZR: Music isn't about having a job and making money; those things are important to survive, but at the heart of it, you're doing it for the love of music. It has value in itself, whether you're creating music or listening to it; there's a reason for it, it's an important part of life.

SIMONE BARON

Photo Credit: Simone Baron

"I'm not exaggerating when I say the accordion saved me—playing phrases on it reminded me how to breathe and sing, reconnecting me and all the disparate parts of my musicianship back to my inner voice."

Simone Baron is a pianist, accordionist, and composer who has performed and toured throughout Europe, America and the Middle East, Canada, the US, and Brazil. She has been awarded residencies and fellowships at the Hambidge Center, I-Park Foundation, Art OMI, Strathmore, University of Maryland's NextLOOK, Avaloch Farm, the Banff Centre, and Spectrum Toronto. In 2016, she founded Arco Belo, a GenreFluid chamber ensemble that dances in the spaces between jazz, avant chamber music, and folk tunes from around the globe. Simone has a commitment to building a more inclusive musical community and is a founding member of the Boulanger Initiative, a DC-based non-profit advocacy group that fights gender discrimination in concert programming. Her multicultural background provides rich soil from which her creativity germinates, and enjoys describing her process as one of decomposition, rather than composition. Her training in piano and conducting at Tel Aviv University and the Oberlin Conservatory gave way to an ongoing love affair with the accordion. When I asked musicians to name influential female performers, Simone's name came up instantly from many of those asked.

SS: Can you tell me how you came to play music and how you found your instrument?

SB: When I was three, I used to fool around with a tiny toy organ for hours, mesmerized by the magic of harmony. I was gifted a small accordion at twelve, teaching myself by visualizing buttons in lieu of counting sheep at bedtime. But I never really had a teacher until much later, so it was sitting there for a long time. At fourteen, I wrote a piece for orchestra and began studying piano. I fell in love with chamber music, with the intimacy of working with a small group to create something poignant but also architecturally sound. By the end of high school, I was practicing fifteen hours a day to prepare for conservatory auditions. Once there, however, I found the environment toxic and became disillusioned. I was so curious and in love with music, so my goal was always to try to understand music from all these different angles—conducting, historical performance, and improvisation. I was very much a dabbler, which was frowned upon by my professors and bewildered my fellow students, and alienated me throughout my academic career. I struggled, developing physical tension (probably some of it was psychosomatic).

By accident, I started fooling around with the accordion again. There happened to be one in the house I was living in one summer. I'm not exaggerating when I say the accordion saved me—playing phrases on it reminded me how to breathe and sing, reconnecting me and all the disparate parts of my musicianship back to my inner voice. After (finally) graduating, I de-educated myself as quickly as possible, leaned into improvising, playing with everyone, and saying yes to every gig, residency, and collaboration. I learned how to channel these disparate genres and experiences into my music—eventually writing, arranging, recording, producing my album, and starting my ensemble Arco Belo. Though I've had a rich and diverse array of musical experiences, my true north are my ears and heart; deep listening and improvising, searching always to be as authentic to the moment as possible. To find musicality and the artistic impulse within oneself, I found it very useful to explore other genres of music and even other ways of making: tension between separate practices creates a point of convergence and departure that holds the artistic impulse taut. For instance, I love working with film and projection, I learn a lot and find I can apply a lot of musical principles to the visual side of it, and once you can get over the technical hurdles of a new medium, it doesn't feel like you're starting from zero at all in it—it feels more like a two plus two equals five situation.

For me, the accordion is a living instrument, a second set of lungs with which I communicate with the world around me. Like lungs, the accordion is influenced by the air it takes in. I often play outside, and watch the sound blossom and evolve depending on the landscape I'm in. Breathing and dream-work are also central to my practice.

SS: What genres do you play—how do they differ/make you feel? Do you have a favorite genre?

SB: I like to say that I make GenreFluid music.

I first fell in love with chamber music in high school. I love the intimacy, the fact that it could traverse so much emotional expressive terrain through form, harmony, and melody. I loved listening to larger-scale orchestral work as well, but chamber music always felt like there was more at stake, you couldn't fall between the cracks.

I guess the great orchestras have this intense potential for overwhelming energy, but it's such a big machine and hard to leverage and needs a lot of things to make the environment right for the power to be unleashed, so to speak, and so often you read about orchestra musicians who are only slightly happier than prison custodians.

Anyhow, I'm not the first person to say it and I certainly won't be the last, but music is a universal language; genres are an invention of capitalism. People need a way to orient themselves around a record shop and identify themselves based on loving everything but what they think is country music or rap, etc., bla bla bla. When you look at the best musicians out there, they are often greatly curious dabblers, some who have reinvented themselves musically many times, and who have not troubled themselves with labels but left it to others. People like Esperanza Spalding, or Hermeto Pascoal, who have such a strong musical identity that by shedding something they become more themselves in this beautiful subtractive shape-shifty process.

There's a great poem by the Sufi poet Hafiz that I set to music years ago that sums up my feelings on genres:

The small man

Builds cages for everyone

He

Knows.

While the sage,

Who has to duck his head

When the moon is low,

Keeps dropping keys all night long

For the

Beautiful

Rowdy

Prisoners.

I started out talking about chamber music—I never said Western classical chamber music, or string quartet—just chamber music. I think chamber music can be a jazz trio, or a rock quartet, or a folk group, and that we probably (uh, definitely) have a lot of weird classist and racist baggage around that... it's no mistake that genre and gender are the same word in my mother language, Italian (and a lot of other languages too). We're in this interesting moment of just beginning to awaken and reconsidering our relationship to gender/binary ways of being, and I think there are a lot of preconceptions of what it means to be a certain gender, just like there are preconceptions about what it means to play a certain genre... As humans, we might enjoy shedding (the "cello goblin" Rushad Eggleston has this great quote on some CD jacket about his favorite snakeskin shedding moment when he stopped caring about genre boundaries). There's something super transgressive about being able to move around these different worlds in the same musical and improvisational space and being able to go really far with your friends playing with you and be like, woah, you know about that too? Woah, you just wanna sit in a hip hop breakbeat for twenty minutes and then do something super contrapuntal? Just like in theater or film, which have this element of catharsis and trying on things in society that you aren't totally ready to IRL (in real life), music is a way to try that on too; what would happen if you could do all that? As long as you can find people who want to go there with you, the sky is the limit. And you can draw in a lot of people too—instead of speaking at a lowest common denominator place, you're challenging people to engage and rise to have a conversation with you, which ultimately is what I want the art I make to do. Genre conventions are boring, they are a starting point, they are the rules of grammar that are made to be broken after you study them.

GenreFluid is my term for this shapeshifting, genre-non-conforming, non-binary music. It is neither classical nor jazz; neither casual nor formal. This music embodies the spirit of the musical polyglot, restlessly searching for the next texture, the next timbre, and the next melody. It is my way of expressing and addressing queer identity and culture.

That being said, I'm a staunch polyglot both in terms of instruments and genres, and try to keep my ears as big and growing as possible. I love getting deep into Western classical music, jazz, folk music, and klezmer, you name it… A deep source of inspiration are hip hop producers, which to me embody some of the best of American music on a somatic, intellectual, emotional, and artistic level. I think J Dilla and Ives should be taught in the same curriculum, and that the satisfying sonic details that can be found on an MF Doom or NoName album can give the Harvard composition department aesthetic a run for its money. Brazilian music also has a profoundly special place in my heart—every part of it is completely dedicated to expressing the full poetic potential of the moment; the melody and the text, and the harmony and rhythm all braid together to serve up the most powerful and simple human expression that reaches every part of your body and reminds me of what I want my music to do too. And, to me, it feels like there's a greater cultural awareness of genre-traversing within Brazilian music. For instance, Guinga… the way he vocalizes his melodies, the unique color of his voice, the crystalline perfect round beautiful tone of every string he plucks on his guitar, I can hear trees swaying and the sun glistening off the top of every bubble of sound, poetry in high definition… there's an artist who is above genre categorization.

I've always identified as a "wandering jew"—and I like to think in a way my music has a diasporic Jewish quality to it—and there's such a history of that in any "genre"—Mendelssohn, Mahler, etc. Growing up in an Italian Jewish household, I listened to some of the great Israeli folk musicians who were very influenced by Brazilian music, and were constantly doing these super interesting harmonic shifts... as well as Italian folk singer-songwriters from whom I inherited a sense of lyricism, storytelling, imagination, and an external reflection/perspective of American music. So hearing Brazilian music later in life and falling as totally in love with it as I did actually made a lot of sense.

SS: As a female, have you ever felt treated differently as a musician than if you were male? If so, can you tell me how and whether you were able to do anything about this?

SB: I am a queer woman, playing a non-traditional instrument in a not quite jazz, not quite chamber music sort of way. To top it off, I'm obsessed with process rather than product, so not everyone understands the value of my work. I can be uncompromising as an artist and in my values; this doesn't always jive with certain spaces and institutions. I want to fight for there to be more inclusive spaces for people like and unlike me.

Of course, I've had my share of discrimination, but I imagine it's not been nearly as bad as it has been for women in previous generations. For instance, I was rejected from a touring grant a few years ago (!) because I happened to have been the third woman from my geographical region to pop up as the panel was evaluating me, and they decided that would have been "one too many women from that region." Or I asked a male musician for a clear and specific contract so that my time was respected and compensated fairly and was subsequently thrown off the project. I know that he wouldn't have treated a male musician the same way. I've gotten called the "b" word to my face by men I've hired and had to fire them, and been in all cis white straight male spaces where I've had to deal with annoying amounts of jokes about genitals and butts because... well... I guess it's hard to be restrained by that shit; masculinity needs its outlets (it was helpful to realize at some point I liked working much more with groups with a minority of guys like that; the humor, focus, and music all get way better immediately). It's mostly ego stuff. There are magnificent men that have been delightful to work with of course too, and are some of my best friends. And even with the men I've had to fire, I've tried to maintain those relationships/friendships when I could and use it as a learning experience and grow from it, rather than cut someone off and write them off for life, which has happened to me and feels absolutely horrible.

Since there are a lot of weird things about me, it's not always easy to figure out what's being discriminated against exactly, and I don't find it the best use of my time to wonder about it if it's not immediately obvious, so I try not to worry too much and try to move on—there are so many super kind people that are also excellent musicians and it's just a more rewarding experience—the more you find them, the more other stuff falls away. Most of the musicians I find inspiring and want to play with or learn from are not like that anyway. I feel like the noise disappears as the music gets better, and if you're not being treated well as a person, you can't be expected to grow musically, so just surround yourself with people that can listen and value you. At least for me, I've developed the way to kind of get a sense of who someone is pretty quickly, and it helps me figure out how to spend my energy appropriately—I think as musicians that's a pretty important skill to have, and it's pretty obvious what someone's ego is like when you improvise or even talk for a few seconds.

This all brings up interesting answers though—the parallels between being a good/kind person and a musician. Can you tell if someone is an a-hole by listening to their music? If you can't but then you know they've done something horrible, do you still listen to them? How do you avoid all that? I definitely know a lot of people who have learned how to pretend/imitate listening in either an improvisational or a notated musical space. To me, it seems really obvious when that's happening and I try to either disrupt it if I can or disengage, when possible, but I guess not everyone can see through that. To be a truly good musician you have to be a deep listener, and that's part of being a good person too, so that all goes together... usually...

SS: Have you ever come across bullying or been bullied in your career as a musician? If so, can you explain this and how it made you feel?
SB: Yes, constantly. Whether it's micro-aggressions of being written off, not called, or having some white guys mansplain my shit to me, having collaborators talk over me or say disrespectful things, or it's being fired for asking to be compensated fairly for my time and asking for a contract, or its weird things people say when I send my music... I've never been the kind of person who can push feelings down, so it's always a little hard to figure out how to manage that kind of negativity—I try to make space to feel it and get it out, and then try to move forward, even if it's fueled by defiant anger for a while.

Even if I know that there are unhealthy things at the root of the issue that mostly have nothing to do with me (insecurity, putting a lot of stock in things that are totally unimportant, working through trauma, etc.), I am energetically very sensitive and have had to learn to find ways to put boundaries down and cleanse myself of these toxic situations. It's been helpful to meet older folks who have had to deal with this for much longer than I have and who just get it and can help put things in perspective. Also, because they paved the way for me to be able to experience this lesser level of that, so I'm so grateful to those generations. I also think it's important to surround yourself with musicians who are kind humans... and it can be healthy and affirming not to always be around straight cis white folks too.

SS: What experiences in music have made you grow as a musician? Were there events that happened which had a profound effect on you?
SB: Being uncomfortable—sometimes the stuff you fail at is a much better lesson than the stuff you excel at.

Also, certain people you play with can change you. Dr. Tyshawn Sorey is an example of that: playing in his large ensemble Autoschediasms at the Banff Centre in 2017 and 2019 were galvanizing, chemical experiences that unlocked new levels of musicality and connectedness in myself each time. In August 2019 I was especially fortunate and got to play a nonstop one-hour concert with a small ensemble coached by/with him at the Banff Jazz & Creative Music Workshop, which may have been the most telepathic, magical chamber music experience I've ever had. The next day we also recorded an hour-long duo album in the dark. Hopefully I'll get to release it at some point. At a certain point, you unlock this level of listening where you completely stop thinking and things happen because they have to and you are just a priestess moving in service to a force greater than you. I've also felt that way when playing in a resonant silo for hours—it's kind of like a drug to be in an environment like that; you start to hear things that were never there before. So things happen in unexplainable synchronicity in those kinds of environments that belie logic. But you have to believe and be open to that kind of magic.

I don't want to paint a picture just of rapture. I've learned a lot from my depression as well. Sometimes I really have to get very stuck and struggle a lot, thrashing wildly among disparate muses until finally accessing what's been inside all along. Sometimes the only way to the other side is through. Sometimes it's just about the consistency of showing up every day and improvising a little, making friends with your instrument first thing in the morning and letting your fingers run, the constant practice of unlearning, surrendering to what my body wants to make—before chiseling, shaping and weaving it, letting it be frustratingly slow, and giving in to time. I saw this sculpture by artist/musician Lonnie Hollie at the Smithsonian the other day, titled "Yielding to the Ancestors While Controlling the Hands of Time." I liked that a lot as a way to describe what composition is like...

But as a performer-improviser, and to some extent any part of music-making, you are an energy worker, and these are the kinds of experiences that have brought me closer to this awareness. It's a special kind of power that can be honed and crafted and "managed" and learned, but if it isn't it can be a very destabilizing force.

SS: Who inspires you? Not just musicians perhaps, but anyone, and can you explain how they inspire you and why?
SB: Beauty. I'm a constant student of beauty. So, I'm really inspired by those who also really love beauty and find a way to capture it, love it, process, and re-express it in this way that just glorifies the original thing. I also love conversations—at the root, music can be a deep conversation with a friend—they are just these journeys where you get to consider all kinds of things connecting and colliding in ways you hadn't considered.

SS: If you had to explain, what would you say music did for/to you? Is there some part it taps into? Does it make you feel emotional? Could it ever be just a job?
SB: Music is a spiritual practice. It's energy work. It's vibration. I think it can take the energy in a room and work with it and change it. It can make the world a better place. It's emotional, it's work, but it's also all-consuming. I see it as magic. You have to work at it. But you also have to believe in it and make friends with it. It's not exactly like a nine-to-five job. But some elements of discipline/consistency are helpful with it. But also it requires a friendship, a relationship, too, based on openness and receiving and listening and trusting, and sometimes even good boundaries. Sometimes it purifies me. Sometimes it gives me a place to cry. Sometimes it makes me dance and gets out this energy that I have nowhere else to put. Sometimes it focuses me and makes me fight in a way that's helpful. Sometimes I can't listen to it.

SS: What would you say to an aspiring female musician? Would you recommend music as a way to make a living? What characteristics do you need?
SB: Keep showing up! The same thing anyone of any gender might need, with perhaps a dash more resilience and gumption. To make a living? I don't know. I think it's worth trying at least. Charisma, kindness, loyalty, consistency, diligence, the ability to listen deeply, open-mindedness, flexibility, creativity, thoughtfulness, patience, are all important and helpful to cultivate as well!

SS: If you had to explain what makes music worthwhile, what would this be?
SB: Too many things to choose from. Listening, opening up doors between people, imagining better worlds, catharsis, imagination in general, constantly being awed by the beauty and gorgeousness that is possible.It just feels like a really important way of processing life and the passage of time.

SS: Do you think the pandemic changed music and how we access it? Or do you think music and how we access it changes over time in any case?
SB: The latter for sure—music is constantly evolving. I think the pandemic made our worlds very small and still (and very big and loud in other ways), but humans have the inherent ability to see beauty and create. I think I've come to appreciate the role of musicians—and artists in general, really—as energy workers, and I've come back to live performance really feeling the intensity of what it means to be in a room with people and have a conversation with listeners. I think the way we listen and the way we relate to other people energetically has shifted in tiny ways, and it's up to us to use it to make the world a better place.

SS: Thinking of that young aspiring musician, do you think it is possible to make a decent living as a musician? How would you advise her to do this and what might her strengths need to be? Does she need to be a businessperson, to plan, get a good manager? What makes the differences between aspiring, struggling and being a success?
SB: I don't know. I think every generation faces unique challenges, and often it can be almost irrelevant for anyone more than five-ish years "ahead" of you in their career/age, give or take, to give a young musician the same advice that worked for them—I think this is actually in a way valuable advice I wish I had had—it frees you up from trying on irreverent models and lets you focus on being the best version of yourself. I do think figuring out your strengths

and developing them is a good idea, finding what you are passionate about within music and how to combine it with your specific skillset. Sometimes it's about a particular collection of interests that are unique to you—maybe other people are good at some of them, but you might be the bridge in between all of that, on your instrument. Or maybe it's an extra thing that's outside of being a musician—i.e., being good at film/photography or physical therapy or some kind of recording production and being able to specialize in helping other musicians because you understand what it's like to be a musician. I know nothing about getting a good manager, as for the type of music I make, I have to manage myself, and anyhow, I think it's important to be able to know how to manage yourself first, so that if someone else ever does, you know how to advocate for what you need/want since you'll understand what it takes and it'll just be nice to delegate things. I think it's really smart in general to be really curious about whatever you need to learn how to do along the way and be open to it, try to learn it as best you can, because you might end up discovering a side passion that will help you and others in your community, and it's always nicer to work with musicians that are interested, curious, asking questions and have professional respect—deconstruct something, learn how to take it apart and put it back together, make friends with it.

Regarding aspiring/struggling/success, I think it's a continuum—you might feel like you're struggling but outwardly look like a success. You're not failing—you're just in the middle of succeeding. In the beginning it feels impossible, the middle slow, and when you're looking back on it, it's gone by way too fast. Your calendar is a better measure than your bank account, and if you think of money as just energy, then if you've already got a lot of that energy, it's only a matter of time before it converts, if that's what you're after. Set yourself up with really good habits—practicing, creating, writing, financial self-care, organization, exercise, and be patient! Also… what is success to you anyway? Is it internally or externally motivated? Is it to be the best musician you can be, play concerts and projects that fulfill you and be able to live comfortably? Or is it to get all of the opportunities you see the next person getting?

SS: How do you see the future for music? How do you see it for female musicians? Have you noticed any positive changes—or not?
SB: Hard to say. Sure, there are tons of incredible initiatives happening everywhere, and I hope they will continue. In just the DC area, there is a women in jazz festival headed by Amy K Bormet, which has been going on for

more than a decade, as well as Dr. Laura Colgate's Boulanger Initiative, which I helped start, which fights gender discrimination in concert programming through education, commissioning and performance initiatives... it's amazing to see things cropping up all over the country and in different parts of the world. Dee Dee Bridgewater's Woodshed Network is also an amazing initiative and holistic model that I was lucky to get to participate in. I hope all these different organizations, residencies, grants, and initiatives can reach enough of a boiling point to last and help build a world where they will someday be unnecessary—the goal is self-obliteration. Also, I think the values/morality in music changes when we start to question the gatekeepers and diversify not only the musicians on the stage but the journalists writing about them, the "judges" and professors at auditions, the orchestral repertoire excerpt composers that are being represented, the presenters, managers, recording engineers, etc., etc.—we have this idea that of what a composer/performer looks like and that needs to be questioned, unlearned and reimagined.

CHARU SURI

Photo Credit: Laura Wheatly

"I love musicians who have an insane passion for what they do and blaze a trail. There are many who say they want to take risks but few who actually end up doing it because it's so easy to play it safe."

Charu Suri is a pianist and composer who blends Indian ragas with other genres. Charu was born in South India and was a piano prodigy performing in various concert halls. Aged just fifteen, she won an international piano competition. She has lived on four continents and her music reflects her traveling and her training in classical music. Her music blends influences from Indian ragas and South Asian Sufi music, Europe, and Africa.

Charu is a voting member of the Grammys (Recording Academy) and has received many nominations and awards as a musician. She has collaborated with the legendary Preservation Hall Jazz Band of New Orleans and played at Carnegie Hall. In The New Jersey Performing Arts Center, the New Jersey Symphony Orchestra played her composition and also her arrangements of popular Bollywood tunes.

Her composition 'Bluesy' won a Band Single of the Year crystal trophy awarded by the International Singer-Songwriters Association (ISSA) in 2021.

Charu has performed at Lincoln Center and other prestigious concert halls around the world, including St. Croix in the U.S. Virgin Islands. She often performs with her band, and sometimes as a soloist. I have enjoyed watching her social media posts about her recent Grammy Awards experience, which proved hugely entertaining. Charu is one of the busiest musicians I know and very kindly took a breather in her schedule to answer my questions.

SS: Can you tell me how you came to play music and how you found the instrument you specialize in? Do you play other instruments?

CS: I was born in India, but my father got a job as the CEO of a record company in Nigeria when I was five years old, and the entire family relocated there. The bungalow we lived in came with an upright Kohler & Campbell piano and I immediately took to it, as my mother said, like a fish took to the water and started playing it and never really stopped. She gave me my first piano lessons and I quickly excelled and started giving concerts from the age of seven.

When I returned to India aged nine, I continued piano lessons with the best teacher in the city of Chennai, and she also taught me to play the veena, an Indian stringed instrument.

SS: What genres do you play—how do they differ/make you feel? Do you have a favorite genre?

CS: I started as a classical concert pianist, and then veered toward jazz only four years ago. I sometimes straddle now with my work between classical/jazz/world and it's hard to really define my music and style.

I have lived on four continents and have a lot of musical influences that I have heard since I was a child—and so many influences and techniques are in the subconscious. Therefore, what I create ends up being an assimilation sometimes of what has bubbled for years. I love classical because of its structure and form. I love jazz because of the improvisation and how it can take you to different moods and places, and I love world music because of the places I have lived in.

SS: As a female, have you ever felt treated differently as a musician than if you were male? If so, can you tell me how and whether you were able to do anything about this?
CS: This is such a can of worms because the answer is most definitely yes, and no matter how much the music world wants to believe that women are getting a fair shake, the odds are really and truly against us.

Almost every single gig I've been on, there's been some sort of comment about my looks and my beauty, and sometimes I'll get a throwaway comment about my music—at least when I was initially starting out. It was really hard to make people respect me for my art, and as I started to progress in my career, then things started to become a bit more equitable.

As someone who has been abused before, I have many scars that I am sure many female musicians can relate to, and I find music is a way to escape my fears, and so sometimes these comments—even though they can seem very innocent—can be extremely triggering, especially as women try hard to get a fair vote in the playing field with men.

Here's an anecdote: I walked into a jazz club last year and the owner was really excited to speak with me and made a lot of comments—"Well it isn't often one gets a pretty lady like you wanting to play"—and honestly that made me squirm a ton inside. Because you know I was there to talk about the music, and it always kept coming back to my looks. And that's the unvarnished truth, and no matter how often I have wanted the conversation to focus on the music, there's always some sort of comment about my being a beautiful woman. So, I have become desensitized to it to the point where I became quite angry about being complimented! Which is ironic I know.

It wasn't until I kept bringing the conversation back to the music and the art that a lot of the musicians that I met initially started taking me seriously. It's a really big issue in the industry! I don't think people realize how serious the scars and the constant belittling can be; it can be a lifetime of trauma. I personally don't find it funny or cute at all. I think this industry can hurt fragile women who are sort of forced to develop a thick skin and condone it, but I don't think it should be condoned.

SS: Have you ever come across bullying or been bullied in your career as a musician? If so, can you explain this and how it made you feel?
CS: Yes, quite a bit. I remember sending my music to a radio promoter a few years ago, and because my music is quite different, his initial reaction wasn't one of surprise at my creativity. Instead, his reply was along the lines of "Well this stuff won't get played on the radio" and I got constantly tired of being told that I couldn't.

There have also been some instances (also I guess because my music is so different from the mainstream) when I sent my first few albums to some clubs for bookings and the response was absolutely rude and horrendous. One agent even hung up the phone on me! But I kept chugging along.

SS: What experiences in music have made you grow as a musician? Were there events that happened which had a profound effect on you?
CS: I have had several amazing epiphanies and moments in my life that have shaped me and my musical vision and voice. One of my earliest memories was learning piano from the legendary instructor in Chennai, India—Mrs. Gita Menon. My parents were so keen to find the best possible instructor there and Mrs. Menon changed the way I thought about music completely. She gave me such a thorough education in both performance and theory, and so many wonderful musical memories came from my disciplined childhood classes with her, including fabulous performance opportunities in some of the best concert venues in India.

Then when I came to the United States to attend Princeton University, I had the great fortune of taking a course with the late great Nobel Prize-winning author Toni Morrison, who had created an "atelier" program at Princeton that paired a composer with a lyricist. Not only did I get to compose my first work for a chamber orchestra, but, as part of the program, both Yo-Yo Ma, the great cellist, and Edgar Meyer, the double bass player, performed my work. It was surreal! I remember Mr. Meyer telling me to never stop composing—that I had a real gift, and that made my year.

That experience had a profound impact on me because I realized that truly great musicians are almost always very humble, and ready to constantly learn.

Another great moment in my life was studying with the great Dutch composer Louis Andriessen, who always told me to trust my ear and my voice. And then four years ago, when I veered toward the land of jazz, I was profoundly impacted by the Preservation Hall Jazz Band and even approached the great drummer Joe

Lastie to be part of my latest album *Ragas & Waltzes* (which he agreed to). After I heard them and their inspired work, it motivated me to do the same with mine.

During my tour in India last fall, I gave a concert at a beautiful Goan café called the Flying Goat, and a young girl who was about twelve years old attended my concert and said it made her day. Quite a few women have approached me from India saying that it is inspiring to see someone who is accomplishing so much and being a female musician from India. There aren't a ton of jazz musicians out there, and far fewer composers who are female.

SS: Who inspires you, and can you explain how they inspire you and why?
CS: I am motivated and inspired by creators of beauty in this fragile and ephemeral world of ours. I really look up to those who go out of their way to create goodness and leave a legacy, because it can be so easy to succumb to hate and damage.

I love musicians who have an insane passion for what they do and blaze a trail. Many say they want to take risks but few end up doing it because it's so easy to play it safe. I get really inspired by those who push the boundaries, especially in music and the arts.

SS: If you had to explain, what would you say music did for/to you? Is there some part it taps into? Does it make you feel emotional? Could it ever be just a job?
CS: Music helps me go places, emotionally. Women get a lot of flak for being too emotional, and I say that's absolutely unfair because we often wear our hearts on our sleeve, and I think that's really healthy—far healthier than bottling it all up inside. Music helps me channel all those emotions. At one concert in the Caribbean, a listener said she was truly transported by my emotional playing and ended up feeling happy, sad, inspired, joyous, and melancholic all in the same concert.

Music has always made me feel emotional: from the very first time that I heard Tchaikovsky to Beethoven's famous *Moonlight Sonata* (to this day I cannot look at the moon without thinking about this piece!). It is quite possibly the only medium that allows me to be my complete self without the need to suppress my feelings. So, I don't think it could be just a job for me, but some aspects of what I do are more banal, like copying parts of scores, etc. But that is largely minimal.

SS: What would you say to an aspiring female musician? Would you recommend music as a way to make a living? What characteristics do you need?
CS: I would say that music is a fabulous way to make a career and the industry really needs female musicians right now, especially more bandleaders and

composers and women who push the boundaries. I would tell aspiring female musicians to follow their voice and their heart, come what may.

As far as characteristics: tenacity is the biggest word that leaps to mind. There are going to be many who will gloss over you and push you aside and not give you the respect that you deserve, but making music and spreading that love to others is honestly what keeps me going. Patience and kindness go a long way too—no one wants to work with someone mean and hard to please!

SS: If you had to explain the one thing (or more) you found which makes music worthwhile, what would this be?
CS: It truly communicates universal emotions and the human condition—it moves me to wonderful levels and is the best therapy I could ever get!

SS: Do you think the pandemic changed music and how we access it? Or do you think music and how we access it changes over time in any case?
CS: Yes, the pandemic definitely changed the way we livestream and the way we access music. It has pushed the way we record for folks watching from home, and I am more mindful of things like microphones and echoes, and lag time when doing livestreams and using platforms like Streamyard to eliminate or reduce compression levels.

SS: How do you see the future for music? How do you see it for female musicians? Have you noticed any positive changes—or not?
CS: The future is and looks truly bright. I am a member of the Recording Academy (often known as the Grammys) which is committed to recruiting more women and diversifying its voting body. I have seen many female musicians step up to be bandleaders and composers and push the boundaries of music, and that has been so inspiring.

Some of the positive changes I have seen is how the music community has embraced the contributions of women. In the last Grammy submission period, I received a lot of praise for my album *Ragas & Waltzes*, and several voting members wrote to me saying they were so happy to see an Asian woman doing what I'm doing. It made me feel so encouraged and loved!

I see many more female producers and bandleaders and composers who are making huge strides in music and doing everything from producing their albums to conducting an orchestra and managing the creative vision—it is extremely inspiring!

SARA SERPA

Photo Credit: Heather Sten

"My biggest wish is that people don't wait for others to create the change they want to see."

Singer, composer, performer, and activist for gender equality in music, Sara Serpa is a graduate of Instituto Superior de Psicologia Aplicada (Portugal) in Social Work and Rehabilitation but finished her studies studying piano and classical singing at Lisbon National Conservatory. She fell in love with jazz and improvisation when she attended the Hot Clube de Portugal's school while working on her research thesis about Refugee Women in Portugal. She relocated to the United States in 2005 to attend Berklee College of Music, followed by the New England Conservatory.

Sara was awarded the prestigious NPR Jazz Vocalist in 2020 and the Female Vocalist Rising Star in 2019 by DownBeat Magazine Critics Poll. She is Artist-In-Residence at Park Avenue Armory, in New York.

She has performed her compositions at festivals and venues across the globe and collaborated with many musicians including Ran Blake, André Matos, Gregg Osby, Ingrid Laubrock, John Zorn, Nicole Mitchell, Okkyung Lee, Linda May Han Oh, Kris Davis, Caroline Davis, Angelica Sanchez, Dan Weiss, Matt Mitchell, Mark Turner, and many others. Sara has performed and interpreted the music of contemporary composers such as Ashley Fure with the New York Philharmonic, Andreia Pinto-Correia, Derek Bermel (with the Albany Symphony Orchestra, conducted by David Allan Miller), Aya Nishina, and Joseph C. Phillips Jr. Sara is also an orbiting member of the performing vocal collective Constellation Chor, a vocal performing ensemble led by Marisa Michelson.

SS: Can you tell me how you came to play music and how you found the instrument you specialize in? Do you play other instruments?
SS: I started playing piano and singing in a choir at the age of seven. I received European/Western classical music training at the Lisbon Conservatory until the age of eighteen. I entered the jazz world in Portugal when I was twenty-two, twenty-three years old and realized this was a free environment where I could explore and create and feel valued. I then moved to Boston, USA, to attend Berklee College of Music and the New England Conservatory.

SS: What genres do you play—how do they differ/make you feel? Do you have a favorite genre and why?
SS: I work mostly in the jazz and creative world, but being in New York allows me to collaborate with many genres, from world music to new and experimental music.

SS: As a female, have you ever felt treated differently as a musician than if you were male? If so, can you tell me how and whether you were able to do anything about this?
SS: I think we are all treated differently, regardless of our gender. What I noticed was that the standards were very high for female musicians—failing meant people talking behind your back about the mistakes made either on

rehearsal, on the bandstand, or just socializing. My behavior adapted to this, which creates some anxiety about failure.

SS: Have you come across bullying in your career as a musician?
SS: Bullying can come in so many ways. I don't think I have been bullied. I think that sometimes bullying in the music world takes place through power dynamics, influence, and gossiping. And this happens without you even knowing about it.

SS: What experiences in music have made you grow as a musician? Were there events that happened which had a profound effect on you?
SS: Moving to the US had a profound effect on the way I saw myself as a musician. I met teachers who were brilliant and encouraging, who gave me opportunities and allowed me to grow in my own way. I was coming from a small scene and was afraid of being different, as many times things tend to be a bit more homogeneous in small countries, where opportunities are scarce and limited. Also, since I started M³ with Jen Shyu, my world has opened up to incredible female and non-binary musicians, who inspire me constantly.

SS: Who inspires you? Not just musicians perhaps, but anyone, and can you explain how they inspire you and why?
SS: Children inspire me (my son in particular!). Their energy, passion, curiosity and creativity make me realize that when there is no judgment, so many great things come out of human beings. And I think that's the energy I always want to cultivate in myself.

SS: If you had to explain, what would you say music did for you?
SS: Music has always allowed me to process the world, emotions, and thoughts, and through it to provide a perspective. It allows me to process the wordless things in life, and I am so grateful to have this way of expression. It is a job, it is a passion, it is a way of life.

SS: What would you say to an aspiring female musician? Would you recommend music as a way to make a living? What characteristics do you need?
SS: I like what the author Sandra Cisneros says: control your finances so you can have creative freedom; control your fertility and make sure you have silence in your life to create.

SS: Do you think the pandemic changed music and how we access it? Or do you think music and how we access it changes over time in any case?

SS: The pandemic moved our lives inward and online, which was a blessing at that time but made us forget the sacred experience that live music is. Things are constantly changing, and more than the pandemic, the online world of social media completely changed musicians' lives. That is sometimes what scares me the most, how it reduces and simplifies our complex human experiences and interactions.

SS: How do you see the future for music? How do you see it for female musicians? Have you noticed any positive changes—or not?

SS: I see a lot of positive changes in terms of gender and racial justice. There is a lot of work to be done, and my biggest wish is that people don't wait for others to create the change they want to see. Institutions move very slowly, but we as individuals have a lot of power together.

RUTH GOLLER

Photo Credit: Monika S. Jakubowska

"What we need is individual voices and to be inspired by each other. I truly believe that if you make honest music, it will be recognized anyway."

Ask musicians to name a bass player and Ruth Goller will be a name that comes up with regularity. Whether soloing or adding rhythmic phrases to almost any genre, Ruth Goller shines like a beacon and has been doing so ever since she appeared on the music scene. She plays jazz, funk, punk, traditional Balkan, Brazilian, and African music, and reggae, and shared a stage with John Paul Jones, Shabaka Hutchings, Sam Amidon, Marc Ribot, Kit Downes, Guido Spannocchi, and many more. Ruth Goller manages to combine a punk style with jazz techniques, proving musicians don't have to make hard and fast choices. She has played with Acoustic Ladyland, Melt Yourself Down, Let Spin, The Golden Age of Steam, and Metamorphic, and released her own albums. Ruth comes from the Italian Alps but lives in London.

SS: Can you tell me how you came to play music and how you found the instrument you specialize in? Do you play other instruments?

RG: My parents always encouraged us to play an instrument. My father came from a musical family but never pursued it professionally. My parents both knew the benefits of children doing something creative. When I was a teenager, I started playing in a punk band, first guitar, then I discovered the bass. I loved the sound of it and found inspiration immediately.

SS: What genres do you play—how do they differ/make you feel? Do you have a favorite genre?

RG: I started playing punk rock but was always into all sorts of music. I then studied jazz, so I have played a lot of jazz and improvised music. I also play a lot of traditional music from all around the globe, but still heavily based on some kind of improvisation. I can't pin it down to individual genres.

SS: As a female, have you ever felt treated differently as a musician than if you were male, or been bullied?

RG: Being female, we are treated differently to males, in life and also as musicians. I have never paid much attention to it and always just reacted to it as to who I am and how I would react in any kind of situation. No, I don't think I have ever been bullied because I am a female musician.

SS: What experiences in music have made you grow as a musician? Were there events that happened that had a profound effect on you?

RG: I find doing last-minute dep gigs, learning lots of hard music for it, and still being able to play well and be professional made me grow a lot as a musician.

SS: Who inspires you?

RG: I've been listening to Björk a lot recently again, and whenever I go back to listening to her music I am completely blown away. She is incredibly inspiring, talented, and innovative. Her music is pure, and the way she can express herself is very clear and honest. I admire that.

SS: What would you say music did for/to you? Could it ever be just a job?

RG: No, it could never be just a job. Even if I had another job (unrelated to music), I would still make music and want to play, I think. For me, playing and writing music is a way of expressing myself, more than I could ever do with words. It's healing for me and helps me to feel balanced and happy.

SS: What would you say to an aspiring female musician?
RG: To a female, as also any other musician, I would say to pursue what they want to say honestly, without thinking about the greater outcome. Without looking for certification from people and the world around you. What we need is individual voices and to be inspired by each other. I truly believe that if you make honest music, it will be recognized anyway.

SS: If you had to explain the one thing that makes music worthwhile, what would this be?
RG: It's a beautiful way of communicating with each other. It's emotional and taps into our deeper souls. For me, more than any other form of art, it is a very direct connection to us.

SS: Do you think the pandemic changed music and how we access it, or do you think music and how we access it changes over time in any case?
RG: Yes, I think music is always fluid and that's the beauty of it too. For me, the pandemic definitely changed things regarding listening and making music, the same as it changed my whole life. I have started to look into things deeper, be truer to myself, be more radical in terms of writing, and ask myself what I really want to do, rather than what I or others think I should be doing.

SS: Thinking of that young aspiring musician, do you think it is possible to make a decent living as a musician? How would you advise her to do this and what might her strengths need to be?
RG: Yes, I think it's possible. I think it's important to always want to learn and be open to improvement. For me, it was important to acknowledge the difference between things I knew I was good at and things I wasn't good at. I still try to improve my weaknesses every day, but I get help with those things if I feel like what I would be doing wouldn't be good enough. For instance, my organizational skills are not as good as I would like them to be, so for me, it's worth employing someone who helps me with that, so I can focus on my work, (writing music and playing). Other people, however, might be good at organizing and not so good at writing, then they would want to get a producer maybe, while still practicing at getting better at writing. I think it's just being real and down-to-earth.

SS: How do you see the future of music? How do you see it for female musicians?

RG: I think the future for music looks great and always will be. It's a strong force that humanity cannot do without. In terms of female musicians, there are so many more female instrumentalists than when I first started playing, and I am really happy to see that. These transitions take time, but I think we are on the right path.

ANJELICA CLEAVER

Photo Credit: Anoush Abrar

"This business can destroy your relationships, your health, and the way you see yourself if you let it."

Angelica "Jelly" Cleaver is lively, colorful and runs events that encourage others to participate in creative arts. She has gained international recognition for her music. She uses music to create community and change. She is Resident Artist at St George's Hospital in Tooting and her creative Jelly's Jams in London provide improvised evenings where artists are encouraged and empowered. She often performs at fundraisers and protests and encourages her audiences to dream of new worlds free from oppression.

Her music style crosses genres, from cinematic and spiritual jazz to raw and rebellious post-punk. She goes from producing hip hop beats to composing contemporary music for piano and projector to playing Jimi Hendrix-inspired guitar solos and leading an all-female disco band. She has worked at underground poetry events and behind DJ decks at club nights.

Her decision to remain firmly uncategorized has seen her receive the Steve

Reid InNOVAtion Award for "outstanding emerging talent," be nominated for an Ivors Composer Award for Large Jazz Ensemble, and be interviewed by the likes of NPR, BBC 6 Music, and Bandcamp.

SS: Can you tell me how you came to play music and how you found the instrument you specialize in? Do you play other instruments?

AC: I started playing guitar as soon as I could hold one. I had to use a capo on the fifth fret so my five-year-old hands could stretch to all the notes. My dad was a guitar teacher, but I think due to his aversion to pushy parents, he never taught me and allowed me to teach myself. Once I'd done all the grades in my teens there didn't seem a further route to go in classical guitar, so I started playing around with an electric guitar, first mostly in a singer-songwriter style, and later finding and loving the sound of jazz. I also had a great music teacher in primary school who taught us the recorder, and I had some piano lessons in my teens. I play bass too and can have a go at most fretted string instruments.

SS: What genres do you play—how do they differ/make you feel? Do you have a favorite genre?

AC: Genre is something I've struggled with, mostly because of industry expectations. I enjoy composing, playing, and listening to as much as possible to grow as a creative, but all the pressure is on pigeonholing you to do one thing, especially if you want to be "successful." I'm involved in the London jazz scene and the punk/post-punk scene, but I also DJ old-school disco and electronic music. I've produced hip hop and soul music. I love playing spiritual jazz but also post-bop and swing. I love heavy music, especially as an electric guitarist. I love playing funky music on bass. I love to compose contemporary classical and experimental music. I love listening to music from different cultures all around the world. I have no idea what kind of music I'll be making in the future either!

SS: As a female, have you ever felt treated differently as a musician than if you were male?

AC: Undeniably. I guess I've always been quite an unusual musician because I'm self-taught and I didn't go through music school like most professional musicians I know, but I really can't imagine half the assumptions people have about me would happen were I male. When I was young and just starting out trying to go to jams, it was very uncomfortable, and I didn't always feel safe. I was usually the only woman, almost without fail the only female instrumentalist. Luckily, in some jams, I'd have one or two older men who looked out for me and encouraged me, but I'd also have to put up with a lot of harassment. I'm also constantly shocked by how far people's assumptions go as a female instrumentalist and producer. This has happened several times—I'll have my guitar on my back, in clear sight, or even strapped to me, and people will ask "are you going to sing?" I'll say, "I'm a guitarist" and the first question most people ask is "do you sing as well?" I'll produce and mix my own music and be very public about my mixing process on social media (videos of me finding sounds, doing nerdy bits, etc.) and people who follow me on socials will ask who produced my music.

I primarily identify as a guitarist, and when I put some music out with me doing a guitar solo, I saw a comment "who's your guitarist, he's amazing?" I've been nominated for an Ivors Composer Award, but I've had several music industry people seem surprised that I can score music. These are literally just the surface of the assumptions that I can see. I can only imagine how many opportunities I miss out on, how many calls I don't get, and how many times I get passed over, because of the assumptions with me being a female musician. And there are so many more micro-aggressions and huge structural issues that I'd need a whole essay to write about fully.

SS: Have you ever been bullied in your career as a musician?
AC: Yes, certainly. It's happened repeatedly actually. It was with people who had a power dynamic over me, and I was bound contractually. In each case, I managed to get out after a long and difficult process, in all cases costing me financially. The abuse of power just creates a huge amount of stress and plays into low self-esteem issues.

SS: What experiences in music have made you grow as a musician? Were there events that happened that had a profound effect on you?
AC: For me, it's been a cumulative process. You always learn from each gig, each jam, and each project. I can't think of any stand-out events. Mostly it's through trying and failing that you learn. And playing with other people, especially in a free or jazz context, can open your mind. The first time I played bass in public was at Moment's Notice, a free improvisation night with Angel Bat Dawid (clarinet, vocals, and pianist) and Mark Sanders (drummer). It was a complete baptism of fire. It went great, and I was never phased playing bass in public again!

SS: Who inspires you and why?

AC: I have so many inspirations. In terms of non-musicians, my biggest inspirations are books. I love to read about activists, science, and philosophy. I get a lot of inspiration from going to protests, talks, and panels. Angela Davis, Fred Hampton, Bell Hooks, Vandana Shiva, Mae-Wan Ho, Frioff Capra, Arturo Escobar, Thich Nhat Hanh, and Adrienne Maree Brown; they're just some of the people who have directly inspired my music.

SS: What would you say music did for or to you? Is there some part of you it taps into? Could it ever be just a job?

AC: At the moment music is my purpose in life and I take that very seriously. Some of the stuff I do I see as just a job, sure. Some is just for fun. But I believe people turn to music for answers, for healing, and connection. They might not even be aware, but when they put on their headphones or buy tickets to a gig, that is what they are looking for. Music is across every culture; it was maybe with humans before language itself; it's immanent in us. And so sometimes I make music for fun, for entertainment, or to pay my rent. But when I make "art," I try to approach that with as much integrity as possible, because I feel music has the power to change us and change the world in some small way, and I think the world needs that!

SS: What would you say to an aspiring female musician? Would you recommend music as a way to make a living? What characteristics do you need?

AC: When I was younger, I had no idea that you could even be a musician unless you were famous. The fact that you could make a decent living didn't occur to me, and I think our society has some very strange assumptions about musicians. I'd recommend they get as much musical education as possible, whether formal or informal. And my main advice is to find your network. Things changed for me when I found my network of predominately female musicians that I could trust. I only really work with mixed or all-female bands, I avoid as much as possible being the only female in a band because I can sense the power dynamics shift, sadly. Get your community of people you trust and bring up other women and gender non-conforming people with you!

SS: If you had to explain the one thing you found that makes music worthwhile, what would this be?

AC: You must find within yourself if it's worthwhile for you, because my experience is that it isn't worth it if you're just thinking about money.

SS: Do you think the pandemic changed music and how we access it? Or do you think music and how we access it changes over time in any case?
AC: I think the pandemic had a big impact on the jazz scene. Jazz is such a lived music, the small jams in sweaty basements or underground venues with musicians coming together and getting that visceral experience with an audience—that for me is what jazz is about. That couldn't happen during the pandemic, and I feel a big shift in the jazz scene before and after. Probably lots of trends happened too. The rise of TikTok. The cost-of-living crisis makes touring unaffordable for many and makes buying tickets to gigs more unaffordable for the audience. Things are definitely changing for the industry, but we've got to keep going regardless, again if it's still worth it for ourselves.

SS: Thinking of that young aspiring musician, do you think it is possible to make a decent living as a musician? How would you advise her to do this and what might her strengths need to be? Does she need to be a businessperson, to plan, and get a good manager? What makes the difference between aspiring, struggling, and being a success?
AC: Yes and no. I wouldn't recommend anyone to become a musician. You've got to feel like there's nothing else you can do. Having said that, there are a lot of ways you can make a decent living! I could give some good business advice, on how to plan your career, build your social media, and get your team. But that quickly becomes how to make your product (your music and you) the most sellable, how to make content (your music) that grabs attention, and how to harness your fanbase, and all these things are counter to what my purpose is in music! Know yourself and know what you're doing it for. If it's making you sad and stressed, hurting your health and destroying your self-esteem (which it sometimes does if you're following the social media formula), get out! This business can destroy your relationships, your health, and the way you see yourself, if you let it. It's dark, but I've seen it happen too many times. You have to work hard and dig deep, search your soul, and stretch yourself, but that isn't "suffering for your art," that's growing as a person. If you're not in the right relationship with music then you won't enjoy making it anymore, and there are probably easier ways to earn money too. Life's too short.

SS: How do you see the future of music? How do you see it for female musicians? Have you noticed any positive changes—or not?

AC: In some ways I think it's a bit easier for the generation coming up now, in terms of gender and gender assumptions being more fluid. There is less binary gender terminology; it's all positive progress. Also, there's more fluidity in the genre, with less emphasis on sticking to traditional boxes of "soul," "rock," "jazz," etc. In some ways, TikTok and social media make it a lot easier to get music out there without the traditional music industry structure. It also changes the focus from being an "artist" to being a "content creator." It's a lot harder to make money in the traditional sense of gigging and selling music. But there are probably new ways to monetize fanbases online with things like OnlyFans and Patreon. I haven't looked into it, but the future's very uncertain and I'm trying to lean into it with a bit of a positive mindset. One thing's for sure, people will always need music!

DESTINY MUHAMMAD

Photo Credit: James Knox

"There are messages in the music, the message that uplifts my spirit and the spirits of my audience. I feel like a conduit of the music, and I love that… Music is my life. It is my all-encompassing lifestyle. Not a job. Music has blessed me to share my life experience with others in a way that is encouraging and inspiring."

With her "Sound Sculptress" identification, Destiny Muhammad has made a huge impact on music. A recording artist and bandleader, composer, and producer, her music is impossible to define, and why would anyone try? Cool, eclectic, a narrative that weaves evocative stories. From cathedral concerts to a San Francisco Symphony series or being a featured guest for Kanye West's "Sunday Service," Destiny has shared stages and musical events with the great and good of many types of music. She has headlined festivals and is constantly in demand. She is Governor Emeritus and Educational Chair Emeritus of the Recording Academy and the American Society of Composers, Authors, and

Publishers (ASCAP) and is a California Arts Council Legacy Fellow.

Destiny was difficult to pin down for an interview, even after she expressed an interest in being part of this book, and I had to wait until she got a break from her hectic schedule. Finally, she managed to work in some quality time to give her considered answers, so I am thrilled to be able to give this interview where Destiny expresses how music has impacted her life.

SS: Can you tell me how you came to play music and how you found the instrument you specialize in? Do you play other instruments?
DM: As a youngster, I sang music I heard on the radio. The Beatles, Johnny Taylor, R&B, and some gospel. Just singing at home. When I was nine years old, I saw the harp on the TV show *I Love Lucy* when Harpo Marx was a guest on the show. I told my mom, "I wanna play harp!" Momz let me know, "That ain't happening! I gotta figure out how to put food on the table!" I let it go. We were struggling to get the basics to live. I finally got my first harp at age thirty, got a teacher, and started studying.

SS: What genres do you play—how do they differ/make you feel? Do you have a favorite genre and why?
DM: My focus is jazz and inspirational music and some gospel. I also play in a community orchestra, the Awesöme Orchestra Collective, with a focus on European classical music. AOC also performs arrangements of R&B and gamer music for the full orchestra. It's fun. These genres feel good to me. There are messages in the music, the message that uplifts my spirit and the spirits of my audience. I feel like a conduit of the music, and I love that.

SS: As a female, have you ever felt treated differently as a musician than if you were male? If so, can you tell me how and whether you were able to do anything about this?
DM: There have been a few times I've been treated differently as a musician—as a woman, instrumentalist, as a bandleader, and as a Black woman on harp. I once hired a bassist to play with me in my trio for a corporate gig. He acted as though it was his date and spoke to me in a condescending manner about the music I had selected and my interpretation of the chord progressions. When the "date" was done, I paid him and deleted his information from all

my contacts. I have seen him out working with other musicians, mostly men. He asked me about playing with him again. I smiled and walked away. I'm not about to entertain drama with him. In my thirty years as a musician and bandleader, I can count perhaps three musicians that have acted salty toward me because of gender. They weren't hired by me again.

SS: Have you ever come across bullying or been bullied in your career as a musician? If so, can you explain?
DM: I was bullied by a woman presenter and producer. She had come to me to be on a women's jazz show she was producing at a local club. She seemed all right and friendly until about a week before the show. She left messages on my services threatening to take me off her show and said I better "act right" or she would make it hard for me to get work anywhere. I felt scared and angry! I had to pull myself together and tell myself I have one God that I live for, and she is not it! I started praying that I remember who I am. I hit that stage with my trio with a cool set of jazz standards. We got big applause from the audience. She came smiling to me after the show, telling me, "Good job!" All smiles. "I have more work for you if you act right." I didn't waste any words on her. I said my prayers, thanked my God, and deleted her information from my contacts. I was told later she was bipolar.

SS: What experiences in music have made you grow as a musician? Were there events that happened which had a profound effect on you?
DM: Coming to the harp as an adult with life experience and coming with the beginner's mindset and being child-like in this respect have helped me to continue to grow. My harp teachers started me from the basics—"Twinkle Twinkle," "Yankee Doodle" and such. It was foundational music.

Most times I was my teacher's oldest student by decades. When I began studying jazz in the Oaktown Jazz Workshop it was the same way. I was the oldest student in classes and workshops—many times learning from my younger colleagues. These teenagers were teaching me, and they became my teachers and mentors.

SS: What inspires you?
DM: What inspires me? Me! It's only by the grace of God that I didn't allow my previous circumstances (growing up in the projects, poverty, divorced parents, welfare) to determine the rest of my life. Those past life experiences

have become navigating tools and sound clips for my musical expression and personal upliftment.

SS: *What would you say music did for you?*
DM: Music is my life. It is my all-encompassing lifestyle. Not a job. Music has blessed me to share my life experience with others in a way that is encouraging and inspiring.

SS: *What would you say to an aspiring female musician?*
DM: What I would say to an aspiring female musician?

- Establish a personal intimate relationship with God as you understand it. I am not talking about religion. I am speaking about your relationship with God/a Goddess or ancestor. It may mean going back into one's personal experiences from childhood—remembering when we would feel the presence of infinity around and within us.
- Learn the basics and study your craft. Apply what you learned. Move beyond theory and move into complete application of the information.
- Learn from the best. I love that the technology is so good you can learn from the best in a virtual class or subscription-based education.
- Listen to the best recordings and go out and hear other musicians. Make the investment.
- Purchase the best instrument you can.
- Celebrate every win, big and small—every win.
- By kind to yourself and everyone. Use wisdom with your words.
- Begin writing your own music. Regardless of where you are in your composing, start now. This includes collaborations with other musicians and songwriters.

SS: *If you had to explain what you found that makes music worthwhile, what would this be?*
DM: What makes music worthwhile to me is the effect it has on ME and those whom I get to share it with! The beauty of the tone and sonic messages coming through are breathtaking.

SS: *Do you think the pandemic changed music and how we access it? Do you think music and how we access it changes over time in any case?*
DM: I sense the pandemic accelerated the way we globally access music.

The pandemic forced creatives of all disciplines to learn new ways to share our gifts with our current audience and develop new audiences locally and globally. Learning to livestream on social media platforms, Zoom, re-stream, and many other things became a necessity. Musicians had to learn how to make live-virtual performances sound, look, and feel good and create revenue streams to keep us afloat. All our in-person performances were canceled. My wonderful husband Cristwell, who is my road manager and harp technician, would stay up late nights online studying OBS (Open Broadcasting Systems) and in chat space on best practices and tools to get the best optimal sound for acoustic instrument livestreaming. We live in Oakland, California—our city is connected with Youth Speaks, a Bay Area-based entity of radical arts technology and social justice innovators, securing them to teach a free eight-week digital course on art and tech basics, livestreaming, available grant opportunities, Adobe, lighting for livestream, and so much! We had to learn new ways to prosper and share our music with the world.

SS: Do you think it is possible to make a decent living as a musician? How would you advise it?

DM: Yes, it is possible to make a beautiful living as a musician and prosper. For me, it required that I recognize that the art of music is a business. I needed to learn how to treat it respectfully.

Some of my teachers and music contemporaries have been very generous in sharing their tips on how to navigate the business side of music:

- Trusting my intuition.
- Being a bandleader (the best I can be).
- Having an accountant and bookkeeper that understands the music business.
- Having a business license.
- Bank account(s) for taxes/expenses/savings/home/investment.
- Joining a music society (ASCAP/ BMI) and Musicians Union.
- Contract creation and negotiations.

In my previous life, I was a barber with a barber shop in Southern California. I gained so many business and life lessons from that wonderful UL occupation! I still apply those lessons to handling clients, band members, and in collaborations. I am a member of InterMusic SF (IMSF), a Bay Area organization that supports musicians with grants, various music business workshops, and performance opportunities. IMSF has a keen focus on the specific creative and economic needs of musicians. I am still learning!

SS: How do you see the future for music? How do you see it for female musicians? Have you noticed any positive changes—or not?
DM: The future of music in my observation is bright. I see musicians and other artistic disciplines collaborating across genres utilizing technology to create and explore ways to share music and arts with our collective audiences/fan base. Musicians are learning to monetize our music in unique ways: podcasts, games, ringtones, and more. Wonderful music relations and collaboration opportunities grew for me during the most aggressive time of the global pandemic (COVID-19). I participated in four virtual residencies! One included a virtual performance at Burning Man! In another residency, I performed virtually for an Indonesian jazz festival, and in another residency with GAMA (Gathering All Muslim Artists), a Ramadan residency that got featured on CNN. I also was a contributor to several music projects and my original composition "Hope on the Horizon" was featured in the Netflix film *Merry Wish-Mas*.

Let me share some of the other groups that assisted in building beautiful connections for my contemporaries, and especially during the pandemic.

MusiCares
Chamber Music America
Intersection for the Arts
InterMusic SF
Musicians Union
SFJAZZ
San Jose Jazz Fest
YBCA
And, of course, so many others!

EMMA SMITH

Photo Credit: Tor Hills

"I do not admire or congratulate the 'struggling artist' rhetoric or lifestyle. I find it quite pathetic."

Emma Smith is packed with energy and talent that she continues to develop and hone. I first heard Emma when I was asked to review one of her albums a couple of years ago, and she has a great voice and delivery. She has performed with some of the biggest names in music and at venues including the O2 Arena, Crazy Coqs, and in New York City. Emma has collaborated and recorded with an impressive array of artists including Michael Buble, Robbie Williams, Georgie Fame, and Seal.

Emma is one of the successful vocal harmony trio The Puppini Sisters, who play across Europe and beyond. She has broadcast on the BBC and received many awards, including the prestigious Worshipful Company of Musicians Medal.

SS: Can you tell me how you came to play music and how you found the instrument you specialize in? Do you play other instruments?

ES: I came to play music through growing up in a family of musicians. The male side—my dad's side—were all brass players, and my grandfather Chris Smith Snr. was an incredibly successful trombonist in that golden era of music-making during the 1960s. He toured with Frank Sinatra for twenty years and played with Sammy Davis Jr., Oscar Peterson, John Dankworth, Tubby Hayes, and more. He was a huge inspiration to me. When I was young, we would sit in the music room of his house—a house he bought after doing a week's work at the Palladium with Shirley Bassey back in the day [laughs]—and he would tell me stories about his career, growing up in the docklands, having absolutely nothing, and how he stole his first trombone and learned how to play it in the woods overnight. He auditioned for the British Army Band Sandhurst and got in and that was it. Years later, he was living in a beautiful huge house making his dreams a reality. We would sit together and study Frank Sinatra's breathwork, and he would tell me how Sinatra studied with Tommy Dorsey, how I should learn to breathe like a trombone player, not a singer. That began my aversion to being called a vocalist and set me on the path of being a singer that could be considered more of a musician than a singer. That really was the beginning of my career.

I play piano, and for a period I played double bass as well. When I was auditioning to get into the Purcell School for Young Musicians, I had to have a third instrument, so I picked up the double bass—for about five minutes [laughs]. I also have a musical mother and a musical father, but really, the story I just told you is how I became a musician.

SS: What genres do you play—how do they differ/make you feel? Do you have a favorite genre and why?

ES: Initially I was really against jazz because it was what took my parents away from me when I was a child. My mum and dad played in the same band, so they were often not at home, and I was brought up largely by my grandmother on weekends and at other times. This was why I spent so much time with my grandfather—who was also out gigging on weekends. So, I had a negative view of and experience with professional musicians in general but particularly jazz and big bands. But when I heard Ella Fitzgerald's version of the Beatles' tune "Can't Buy Me Love," my preferred genre of rebellious rock and roll went almost instantaneously from the Beatles to Ella Fitzgerald. It was the sound of the big band that filled me with excitement and joy. And now, just being in front of a big band, having that wall of sound behind you, kind of propelling you to energize an audience is what most inspires me. Big band swing, Sinatra, and all that stuff is my favorite genre [laughs].

I went to the Royal Academy of Music for four years to do a degree, and after playing a lot of free jazz there—which was essential to my development as a musician—I massively rebelled against that and got into pop music—relatively left of center pop music—but I did a lot of writing and released music under a different name. The name was ESPA, which I used to joke about. When people asked me what it stood for, it was Emma Smith, Piss Artist, but it was a derivative of an ancient Jewish name, Esme—or Esther. Esme, Esther, and Emma are all variations of the same Hebrew name. I had some very interesting experiences when I was in the pop world—being a female in a world that had a lot of females—as opposed to something like jazz, which has not so many.

SS: As a female, have you ever felt treated differently as a musician than if you were male? If so, can you tell me how and whether you were able to do anything about this?

ES: The big answer is "yes," but I want, if I may, to take this opportunity to talk about my mother. My mum is a brilliant lead alto player. She grew up desperately trying to get hold of a saxophone in the 1970s. The bulk of her career was in the 1980s. My mother came from a very poor family in Romford and was horrifically bullied because of her race. Her escapism was music and she got really good. She played lead alto with that classic Glenn Miller sound. She would send off audition tapes. Her name is Simone, and, if you take the "e" off the end it reads "Simon." She would do that for her audition tapes and instantly get called in for a trial. My mum has told me many stories about turning up for trials with those bands, such as the Glenn Miller Band and Ray McVay's big band and other dance bands at the time, and, as she walked in and they realized she was a female musician, they would ask her to either leave or ask her to begin to dress provocatively. She had it said to her face that they would rather have a cardboard cut-out than a female musician, regardless of how brilliant she was. She even once went on stage with a fake mustache, a suit, and her hair pulled back. It really was that bad for her.

I have also had experiences of being treated differently as a woman, but growing up, having my mum's experiences in the back of my mind, it has never felt quite as horrific. It seems to be so ingrained in the culture. I am not only a female musician, but I am also a female singer who is as capable as any musician in terms of my knowledge of harmony, history, charts, conducting, etc. Yet I have had the issue of being a "turn." "Come on stage, give us a twirl, and wear a nice glittery dress!" I have been patronized my whole life. It makes me feel quite angry and I can feel it bubbling up even now as I speak to you. That sense of frustration, of being patronized and treated like a useless ornament to the music. Isolated away from the musicians and their talk, which is almost what has fueled me to study techniques such as Maggio and Caruso for trumpet players, which I studied not just to enhance my breathwork but to enable me to surprise musicians with my knowledge of their instruments and how I can use their tools.

I have done many transcriptions and I have knowledge of other musicians; for example, all the transcriptions and studies I have done on musicians including Dexter Gordon. I like to keep it to myself until they patronize me and then I pull it out.

SS: Have you ever come across bullying or been bullied in your career as a musician? If so, can you explain this and how it made you feel?
ES: I was bullied at the Royal Academy of Music. I was the only girl in my year of eight students. Across the entire board of students, including four years and two years post-grad, I was, for a period during my undergrad studies, the only girl on my course, and I was bullied.

When my boyfriend and I broke up, his friends took that to heart. One morning I arrived at college and there were pictures of me on fliers everywhere with a "no entry" sign across my face. These had been distributed across the college and it was horrific. A lot of the tutors knew what was going on. Nothing ever got done about it. In fact, some tutors would be going for pints after classes with the students that were putting the fliers round—fliers that said "no entry" for me at the college that I was paying a lot of money to be at. It was horrific. I do understand there is a gray area with students and tutors at conservatoires—because they may end up playing the same gigs—and this did happen. You end up being friends with them and you leave college, and you are still friends with them. This is the case for me as well, but at the time I feel there was a line that became incredibly blurred. This was from 2009 to 2013, which isn't that long ago, and I feel things should have been handled differently, as I was made to feel incredibly isolated when I was at the Royal Academy of Music.

There have also been many occasions when I have felt bullied. In NYJO (National Youth Jazz Orchestra), when I was there from 2006 to 2012/13, me and the flutist were the only girls and there was a lot of catcalling and misogynistic comments consistently from the band—and the bandleader! I noticed some appalling stuff happening when I was there. I am sure it has been tightened up and is dealt with differently now, but I sat in that very funny niche gray area where things went from the 1990s/2000s way of how females were treated in bands—which was better than how my mum was treated but still quite bad—to where now all of a sudden it seems quite different.

SS: What experiences in music have made you grow as a musician? Were there events that happened which had a profound effect on you?
ES: This question brought something to mind I often think about. I was fifteen years old and touring with my grandfather's big band, the String of Pearls, and to soundcheck the microphones of the singers I had to sing four notes—one, three, five, and flat seventh. I couldn't pitch the flat seventh. My grandad asked for a dominant seventh arpeggio. I couldn't pitch it and he put me on the flat seventh. My grandfather wasn't a gentle man; he was a very tough man and his nickname in the industry was "the Rottweiler." Even with his granddaughter, it didn't change things in a professional setting—he was as loyal as anything but could be brutal. I was humiliated by not being able to pitch the flat seventh, and he kept saying, "Go again, go again, go again!" and this was in front of a sixteen-piece big band of middle-aged and older. I went home that night, and I don't know at what point I fell asleep, but I continually sang over and over one, three, five, flat seven, one, three, five, flat seven until it stuck, and it has never left my mind. That experience changed my life. It was traumatic, and it meant that my skin thickened, and I never wanted to be embarrassed in front of a room full of middle-aged men again—and I never have.

SS: Who inspires you?
ES: People who inspire me are women like Vivienne Westwood and Iris Apfel, ironically both in fashion and styling. I love dressing myself. I find it to be such

a tangible expression of how I am feeling and who I am. My wardrobe is like a color explosion, and it cheers me up, it excites me. I find it rebellious in its silence. Artists like Vivienne Westwood have paved the way for women like me who are full of anger and rebellion to express that in a way that doesn't necessarily get them into trouble. I wear certain quotes of Westwood's on tee shirts that could get me in trouble because they have swearing on them, or Malcolm McLaren's "Cash from Chaos." I wear another that says "Bombing for peace is like fucking for virginity." For me, I find it freeing and empowering. I have tattoos of both Iris Apfel and Joni Mitchell—Joni sits in that same world, she smells the same as Vivienne, who will join my hall of fame of tattoos soon. Joni Mitchell is a singer and woman who just holds so much rebellion and quiet self-awareness and power. She is so respected and aspired to.

Another musician I admire is Barbra Streisand—as a singer and actress spanning Hollywood. To be able to have Oscars and Grammys is just inspiring to me, but beyond that, it is the grace with which she holds herself and the respect her demeanor and aura just simply demands. Her elegance and artistry are incredible, I find her fascinating. Plus, the fact she is an out-and-out proud Jewish woman for me is the ultimate goal in terms of respect and admiration.

SS: If you had to explain, what would you say music did for/to you? Is there some part of you it taps into? Does it make you feel emotional? Could it ever be just a job?

ES: This is so interesting. I feel this extreme tug of war within myself, which is the crux of the reason I did music in the first place. It was absolutely necessary. It was emotional, it was animalistic, and essential for my survival. Having been doing it professionally for seventeen years now, since I was fifteen, it does sometimes feel like a job. I don't think either is bad. I think when it becomes just a job it is a problem and when it becomes all about identity and emotion it is also a problem. I struggle to create a healthy balance of the two because I don't feel music is something where you can control the way it makes you feel—yet in the same breath, when you lose that feeling, it is not worth doing it.

There have been phases in my life when I felt it was just a job—and this has always been because of the setting. Going around the restaurant-bar scene and cafes singing the Great American Songbook seven nights a week for really low fees just to pay the rent, with an audience that doesn't clap between numbers, so you develop a technique with your pianist where he launches into out-of-time music a tritone away from the key to fill the gaps so you don't have those awkward silences—it can get a bit soul-destroying. At times I have taken on non-musical roles to fulfill that "I need money" criteria. And yet, when I have made it all about emotion, such as when I had vocal health issues, which I have had all my life—I had two lots of surgery, which left me unable to sing for four months at a time and not even speak for the first six weeks—I have felt so empty and like I was emptied of my identity because music and being a singer is who I am. I am someone who expresses themselves through music and touches others and thrives off that audience–artist experience. Being left without that and the prospect of not being able to do that so regularly is worrying because you have the thought, "Wow, I have allowed music to become my number one identity before being a human with relationships." I actually feel—and this might seem crazy or sad—but my relationship with music goes deeper than my relationships with most people.

Of course, relationships with family and partners ebb and flow—from being full and romantic to being full of logistics, and that is exactly what happens with me and the intangible music. The fact that when I first read your question, the first sense I had was bubbling emotion, leads me to believe that the intangible, spiritual, magic of music (gee I sound so pretentious [laughs]) is triumphant above anything.

Something more on how the emotional side of things can work. Recently I released my album *Meshuga Baby*, which featured a very slow version of Shirley Horn's "There's No Business Like Show Business," and when I sing that song and explain to an audience that the words are so potent—for example "there's no people like show people, we smile when we are low"—that simple lyric and an audience understand the potent message I am delivering, I allow myself to sink into the music and the message and let the music pour out of me. On recent gigs, I have seen grown men bawl their eyes out. It makes me emotional even speaking about it. There is an area of the heart and the soul music taps into, and combined with lyrics, it is powerful, healing, and moving, and can stir even the most thick-skinned of our community. I mean, grown-assed men sitting there with their wives and family, wiping their faces as they are moved and become aware of the human experience. For me, this is like a drug. I can't let go, and it soothes my soul to connect with people I have little in common with. For me, that is absolutely magical.

SS: Thinking of that young aspiring musician, do you think it is possible to make a decent living as a musician? How would you advise her to do this and what might her strengths need to be?

ES: I think it is possible to make a fantastic living as a musician and I am proud that I have been doing this since I was fifteen years old. I think this is down to diligent studying, having a voice, having a business mind, being fearless and being braver in communication—such as speaking to the guy who has worked for a promotions company for twenty years and having the confidence to sell myself to him as an artist. This has not always been the case and still is not always the case, but I think if I am feeling insecure about anything I am doing, the confidence that I have felt in the past helps me access it again.

I would not deter someone from making a living out of music, but I would say that to do so and survive as a musician—and I guess I am talking specifically to singers here—don't even attempt this in the jazz world or the non-trashy pop world without having watertight musical chops. Get your technique down, your theory down, your harmony down, your knowledge of chord changes down, your knowledge of the language with which to direct and explain to a band about the geography of the Great American Songbook—your awareness of the history of jazz, your transcriptions, your bebop knowledge. Just commit to doing it properly or don't bother, because you will be laughed out of any band room ever—or perhaps not and you will just be talked about behind your back, and that is not sustainable. I would also say you have to have immaculate business chops and skills and have your savvy head on socially so you can talk both to musicians and clients or venues because you will be the person arranging most things. Also have a quiet awareness that as a musician fronting a band, you are the one that is going to sell most tickets. You are the one most promoters need—know that deep inside of you and understand you have power and are important. Once I understood that, it freed me from a lot of desperation of wanting to be included in the lad culture—certainly with big bands.

SS: Do you think the pandemic changed music and how we access it? Or do you think music and how we access it changes over time in any case?

ES: I am so allergic to the plastic pop music we hear on the radio—it does nothing. It is produced and processed to the point the soul is removed, and I find this cynical. I noticed post-pandemic that pop music used a lot of reworkings of older songs people would know. The songs are being recorded using singers, some of whom I know—and session singers as they cannot get hold of the masters. They are putting them in house-style remixes. It is going wild because people were craving comfort during the pandemic and because they already know those songs. So, they get remixed, and they make lots of money. I find it cynical. I have noticed that post-pandemic there are extremes. There are those who want unchallenging music and TV or there is the opposite side where people are buying vinyl, going to the theater, and watching live music, so I think the middle has fallen out—the average, cross-spectrum has exited the landscape, and we are left with either processed trash or chin-stroking, challenging art. Which is slightly worrying.

SS: What makes the difference between aspiring, struggling, and being a success?

ES: I do not admire or congratulate the "struggling artist" rhetoric or lifestyle. I find it quite pathetic. I find it sad and damaging. It discourages people from moving forward with their art. For me, when I was a struggling artist, I got a job. I met non-musicians and applied myself to a non-musical role, an admin role. I found it invaluable to the way I now operate as someone who books a lot of musicians every month, books lots of engineers, and talks to PR people and interviewers, for example. I don't just surround myself with musicians, and I think having a "normal" job (a "muggle job") is healthy, and necessary even to being a successful musician in the world.

SS: How do you see the future for music? How do you see it for female musicians? Have you noticed any positive changes—or not?

ES: I have noticed that right now female musicians are being tokenistically booked, and I think that is interesting. I do not think that is necessarily a bad thing if they are brilliant musicians who have not had a platform thus far in their careers. I do think it is a bad thing if they are not accomplished musicians or not "cooked," not ready yet. I notice some young musicians are very ready, very capable, and some who are not. Some young musicians who are not ready are being put on too big a stage, too big a platform, too soon for the sake of fulfilling diversity quotas, and I think that can be damaging. However, I do think the efforts of promoters and festivals to book more female musicians are brilliant, however transparent. I think the playing field should remain equal, so it doesn't feel to female musicians that this is just a flash in the pan. We need to believe the music industry is committed to platforming and highlighting equal opportunities for all races, all sexes, and all people from all walks of life moving forward, not just a couple of years of female-only-led festivals. I am concerned about that.

I do worry too about the mental health of my male colleagues because of the influx of tokenistic bookings of females and the desperate attempt of venues and festivals to not be canceled for not booking females. There is now a neurotic panic and fear among men who have had an absolute monopoly over the field over the years. I am not saying they shouldn't have fewer gigs, but they also shouldn't have *no* gigs and *no* platforms. So, I shall watch with interest how the landscape changes and will try to keep myself going in the same way as I have done.

I do not trust that the opportunities will grow without my efforts, and I do not think any other female musician should trust that either. That might be cynical, but unfortunately, cynicism is helpful. It has helped me in my career, and it helped my mum to make a living as a saxophonist. But none of it has been without our incredible efforts and commitment to the music and the business—and to always get better as musicians.

COLLETTE COOPER

Photo Credit: Blake Ezra

"There are no rules! Be yourself, which is very important!
Take inspiration and influence but never emulate!"

Collette Cooper is an actress, singer, and producer. Signed to Thelonious Punk Records, she has appeared on the BBC, Soho Radio, and Jazz FM. She has sold out many venues and shared the stage with KT Tunstall and Texas. She is also an activist and artist. Her work has appeared in The Now Exhibition curated by Leah Wood. Collette also broadcasts a podcast series Sisters in the Shadows *that highlights female musicians, producers, and artists. Her portrayal of Janis Joplin in the play* Tomorrow May Be My Last *at the Old Red Lion Theatre in London gained critical acclaim.*

SS: Can you tell me how you came to play music and how you found the instrument you specialize in? Do you play other instruments?

CC: I guess I've always sung one way or another since I was little. Both my parents like to sing, and my brother, too, is a musician. My dad bought me my first keyboard when I was nine, although I specialize in vocals, but I do like to tinker on the piano and guitar, and it's useful for writing.

SS: What genres do you play—how do they differ/make you feel? Do you have a favorite genre and why?

CC: I'm definitely a blues gal! I'm influenced by jazz, blues, and even classical, but blues is firmly in my soul. It's the music I was brought up on. My dad introduced me to great music and artists. Bessie Smith is one of my ultimate heroes. She was raw and honest. She sang with truth.

SS: Have you ever felt treated differently as a musician because you are female?

CC: I've never really experienced any discrimination as a woman, maybe because I'm quite a forceful character and I definitely wouldn't stand for that. I only experienced one incident with a male friend I brought on board one of my projects, but I think it was more down to the fact we had very different musical backgrounds and there was a clash, but we soon sorted it out after I had a good screaming match, LOL :) I think as a woman you need to stand your ground in any industry. But my pet hate is pulling out the "I am a woman" card. Sometimes I think men just like to be overprotective. It's in their nature and sometimes that attitude rubs women up the wrong way. It's not always sexism, and I feel men get a bad rep sometimes. When I work with guys, we just become a team and get on with it.

SS: Have you ever come across bullying or been bullied in your career as a musician?

CC: Not really, however, I wasn't really impressed with a male engineer once at a recording studio who asked me to get the producer in, and I had to remind him that I was the producer! I felt his attitude was a little disrespectful, but again, you just need to stand your ground. In retrospect, part of me wishes I'd fired him, because he wasn't cheap and neither was the studio. Needless to say, I would never record there again!

SS: What experiences in music have made you grow as a musician? Were there events that happened which had a profound effect on you?
CC: I grow and learn every day! I think the longer you do it the more comfortable you become in your skin. I have so many events that have had a profound effect on me. One that stands out is the concert at the Roundhouse I did along with Chrissie Hynde and Bob Geldof and many more in March 2022 to raise money for Ukraine.

SS: Who inspires you? Not just musicians perhaps, but anyone, and can you explain how they inspire you and why?
CC: I'm inspired by many wonderful people in my life, including my dad, my brother, and my whole family. I'm fortunate enough to have a wonderful and extremely kind family who brought me up to understand the importance of helping other humans along the way while being on our own journey. Kindness is everything! And my partner Mike inspires me every day! He's a great musician, he's a kind soul, and has a great outlook on life!

SS: If you had to explain, what would you say music did for/to you?
CC: Music is everything to me! It heals me! For me, it's the best job in the world! I'm so looking forward to getting back into the studio this summer, which is Dean Street Studios in Soho. Can't wait!

SS: What would you say to an aspiring musician?
CC: I'd say just do it and learn on the way! There are no rules! Be yourself, which is very important! Take inspiration and influence but never emulate! Be your own unique self!

SS: If you had to explain the one thing that makes music worthwhile, what would that be?
CC: Simple. The rollercoaster of emotions it brings to you and others. Utter joy!

SS: Do you think the pandemic changed music and how we access it? Or do you think music and how we access it changes over time in any case?
CC: Yes, the pandemic changed a lot of things, but the world is evolving constantly anyway, and we just go with it; it's evolution! Get your music out there any way you can.

SS: Do you think it is possible to make a decent living as a musician? What advice would you give to an aspiring musician?

CC: There are definitely more struggling musicians out there than well-established ones, but keep going! It helps to have a manager, so you can just focus on the art, but it's not necessary. Success doesn't always mean huge fame and fortune. You are successful if you are making music and performing it. Just don't give up. The fact that you don't give up and you keep going is a huge success in itself.

SS: How do you see the future for music? How do you see it for female musicians? Have you noticed positive changes?

CC: Female musicians are getting more visual and even stronger and stronger. Music will always prevail; it's music! It doesn't have a lifespan; it'll keep going way beyond our lifetime.

EMMA RAWICZ

Photo Credit: Courtesy of Yolanda Drake Awards. Photographer: Mariola Zoladz

"To become a financially successful musician a lot of things need to fall into place. You need to be a businessperson. You need to plan; you need to be organized and you need to understand that your relationships with other people play into what you are then able to do creatively."

I first heard Emma Rawicz when I watched the final of the BBC's Young Jazz Musician of the Year in 2022. I was struck by her intuitive playing and also her engagement with the other musicians on stage accompanying her—and she was just twenty years old. Since then, Emma has sold out venues like the prestigious Ronnie Scott's in London and won a Parliamentary Jazz Award. She has already been nominated for numerous prestigious awards and played at major festivals internationally. The fact that at such a young age her quintet features incredibly talented musicians such as Ivo Neame, Conor Chaplin, Ant Law, and Asaf Sirkis, with guest vocalist Immy Churchill joining for her recent release, demonstrates the respect this musician has already achieved. She recently signed to the prestigious ACT label and her star is most definitely in the ascendant.

SS: Can you tell me how you came to play music and how you found the instrument you specialize in? Do you play other instruments?

ER: I don't think there is a specific answer for how or when my journey in music began. I know that I have been fascinated with music from an early age and was eager to get my hands on any instruments around me. I can remember messing around with instruments like the guitar and piano from when I was about three years old or even younger. However, when I was about six, I picked up a violin and began practicing with a bit more direction. It took me quite a while to find the saxophone and the jazz genre—which is where I "hover" stylistically these days. Mostly, this was due to the fact I grew up in Devon and there was little live music, but I felt a strong connection to the instrument, and it had been an ambition to play the saxophone for a long time before I finally got the chance when I was aged sixteen. I continue to play a variety of instruments. I think being a multi-instrumentalist can be a strength in a variety of ways. Even if it can just provide you with different sounds and give you a different viewpoint on even the same piece of music, so I taught myself the flute. I play the clarinet and bass clarinet and a bit of piano, and very privately I sing a little bit, although that is a bit of a strange one for me because, as a female musician, I have found, especially in the jazz genre, that sometimes if you are a singer and you also play other instruments then for some reason your instrumental ability might be taken less seriously. So, I play other instruments and have been playing the saxophone for around five years.

SS: What genres do you play—how do they differ/make you feel? Do you have a favorite genre and why?

ER: The genre I mostly play or inhabit I would say is jazz, though I guess what I do can be categorized in a number of ways and can loosely be called improvised music. There are tons of different genres and types of music that feed into what I do. Music such as rock music, folk, funk, and classical music—which I played mostly when I was younger—has fed into the music I write and play. I don't think it is possible to say I have a favorite genre because in a lot of ways I think genres can be constraining as much as they can give you direction, so I try not to think much about this when I play. I try to look objectively at what I have made at the end of the process. I guess I would call myself a jazz musician if I had to choose.

SS: As a female, have you ever felt treated differently as a musician than if you were male? If so, can you tell me how and whether you were able to do anything about this?

ER: As a female, I do believe there are and have been situations in which I feel I have been treated differently from male colleagues. Most of this has been quite subtle. For example, I feel there have been situations in which men mostly have assumed my technical ability on my instrument or my knowledge of the history of jazz would be weaker. It is difficult to know what to do about this. I believe that particularly when dealing with musicians of the older generation there may be no malice at all, and in fact, it might be misguided good intentions to treat you differently as a female, but there is the odd and unfortunate situation when there is malice involved and someone is trying to make you feel small or less valued because you are female, so it is important to find a way to call them out on their actions and ask them why it is they are treating me differently. It is a tricky topic though, because you can easily imagine issues or malice when there isn't a problem purely because it is very easy to feel self-conscious when you are the only woman in the room or one of very few. So, I guess the only thing to do is to keep the conversation going and keep male friends and colleagues appraised of how you feel, what is going on in your head, and how the situation comes across to you. I have found that sometimes from a male musician's perspective they either haven't thought about it like that or there was zero intention from their viewpoint.

SS: Have you ever come across bullying or been bullied in your career as a musician? If so, can you explain this and how it made you feel?

ER: Within the music industry, it would be naïve to deny the existence of bullying. I think I have experienced this once or twice, but it is not something I spend a good deal of time thinking about. Most of the time, I feel it is important to show people you won't be walked all over, for want of a better phrase. Bullying exists because of insecurity, in my opinion, and once you realize this, it can be very freeing. You are not the problem. Stand your ground and let the music do the talking!

SS: What experiences in music have made you grow as a musician? Were there events that happened which had a profound effect on you?
ER: There have been many experiences that have made me grow as a musician. I think one of the most profound changes I noticed in myself as a musician or creative person was when I put myself in situations that frightened me, or more specifically, when I began to play with musicians older and more established than myself. I found this a natural and organic way to learn first-hand how to grow as a creative person and interact with people. I am very lucky to have been able to record an album with some of my heroes of the UK jazz scene, and the entire process of that was huge for me. In general, I think that endeavoring to spend time around more experienced musicians and learn from them in the most organic way possible is the most effective way to grow.

SS: Who inspires you? Not just musicians perhaps, but anyone, and can you explain how they inspire you and why?
ER: When asked who inspires me, the first person I think about is Maya Angelou. I find her response to adversity in so many situations really heartening and inspiring, and it makes me want to be a better person and embrace my creative life and try and flourish in that too. She was an incredible writer and person. Having read most of her autobiographical books, I get a sense of who she was as a person, and it touched me on a deep level. It encourages me to be a better person, not just a musician. Musically, the list could go on forever, but people I am finding particularly inspiring creatively at the moment are Marius Neset, an incredible Norwegian saxophonist, and, going back a bit, Joe Henderson.

SS: If you had to explain, what would you say music did for/to you? Is there some part it taps into? Does it make you feel emotional? Could it ever be just a job?
ER: I would say music gives me a chance to be outside myself in the most positive way possible. I would say, in daily life, it is easy to go along and get caught up in trivial everyday matters, just like everyone, but as soon as I get to play music or listen to music, especially when I play with the right people, it transports me—and I think this is a common thing with many musicians. It taps into a real raw emotional part of a person, and obviously that is experienced differently by everyone, but I feel lighter when playing music. I do not think music could ever be a job, or if it did end up feeling that way, I would feel sad because most of the time, especially when playing my own music, or original

music by others who inspire me, it feels like I am incredibly lucky to be able to call this my "job." I don't feel it would ever be right to just go through the motions when playing music, so that is something I try to avoid. I know I am lucky to be able to do as much work as I feel creatively stimulated to do. For me, I would rather do something completely unrelated if I needed something that was just a job outside music. I think that might be better for my soul.

SS: What would you say to an aspiring female musician? Would you recommend music as a way to make a living? What characteristics do you need?
ER: I think the advice for most aspiring musicians regardless of gender would be the same. When it comes to separating people and marking them out because they are female, I think that can sow the seeds of problems later on, because I feel we should be aiming for a world where everyone can play music and doesn't experience any issues because of their gender or anything else. I would say to anyone that music—if that is what you want to do—requires commitment. Even more than that perhaps, it requires you to be able to form meaningful and positive relationships with other people—unless you are going to be a concert pianist who only performs solo recitals, and even then, you need to have a decent skill set when it comes to being able to communicate positively with others, especially when dealing with fellow creatives. I think the best art or music is created when people can connect in a positive way on a human level. I wouldn't necessarily recommend music as a way to make a living unless someone was in a situation where they felt they were doing themselves a disservice if they did not pursue a music career, because of the inevitable low points or more difficult times. There really is a deep and powerful passion for the music required to carry you through those times and maintain a positive association with music, otherwise it is easy to become disillusioned and lose sight of the point of making music at all.

SS: If you had to explain what makes music worthwhile, how would you do this?
ER: I don't think music, in itself, needs to be made worthwhile. Music is and will always be what it is. As humans, we get to partake in it and create it, but ultimately, once it is made, it can exist without us, and even without humans, music exists in the world in all sorts of ways. One of the things I find valuable about music is how it can unite people beyond politics, language, region, or anything else. Music can trigger a visceral, emotional response that cannot be translated into words, and that is something precious in my opinion.

SS: Do you think the pandemic changed music and how we access it? Or do you think music and how we access it changes over time in any case?

ER: I think the pandemic had a hugely negative impact on the way we access music. I guess it changed music in that less of it was being created live in a room with others. So much of what makes music special is the ability to connect with other people. When people are in a room together creating music, something magical can happen. To deprive a lot of people of that was really damaging, not just to musicians but to everyone who consumes music and is made to feel something by music. It made the way we access music more virtual. I am not an advocate of a lot of screen time, so that isn't a good thing in many ways. I do think it was great that it was there because it was a time when we all needed a lot of support mentally and emotionally and being able to access music that made you feel comfortable or feel connected with other humans that you weren't close to physically, that was a valuable thing in the circumstances. However, I think it has meant there has been slightly less support for live music on a large scale. I think that, individually, people wanted to get back out and support live music and the musicians that enable that to be available to them. However, I think venues and some people are a bit tentative still. It is improving, but it has created a kind of tentativeness and an unwillingness to commit to putting on live music. That can be damaging to the general situation for musicians. I do think how we access music will change over time. I hope with all my heart that we will continue to value live music and how special that can be, particularly as a musician who plays music that is heavily improvised. The beauty of live music is that you are partaking in an experience that is completely unique and can never repeat itself. This simply cannot happen without live music, so I hope that as a species we continue to appreciate and support this. However, the next Spotify may change things fundamentally. Alternatively, we may all stop using Spotify, Apple, or streaming services and go back to buying CDs. Who knows? There is no way to plan for this, so I guess we shall just have to wait and see.

SS: Thinking of that young aspiring musician, do you think it is possible to make a decent living as a musician? How would you advise her to do this and what might her strengths need to be? Does she need to be a businessperson, to plan, and get a good manager? What makes the difference between aspiring, struggling, and being a success?

ER: To become a financially successful musician a lot of things need to fall into place. You need to be a businessperson. You need to plan; you need to be organized and you need to understand that your relationships with other people play into what you are then able to do creatively. It is definitely possible to make a decent living as a musician. It depends on where you live, whether that is in a city or more rural, and can come down to which country you live in and how much funding is available for the arts in that country. I don't think management is necessary, but it all depends on the kind of person you are. It also depends on which avenues within the music you would like to go down. The chances are high that you may need to be able to do a huge mixture of things. You may need to write music, or you may need to teach, you may need to do functions, you may need to arrange music for other musicians, and all alongside doing live gigs. You might want to do sound—there are so many ways you can have a successful and fulfilling portfolio career, and I think one of the mistakes people make is to think they need to be doing a certain number of live shows per year or month to be successful and that is just not realistic, or something that even applies consistently to a group of even similar people. The difference between aspiring, struggling, and successful can often be based on luck and being in the right place at the right time. However, I genuinely think that with continued effort and commitment something will stick at some point, and sometimes you need to be prepared to veer off course and take a slightly different route to your end destination than you had planned, perhaps taking a second job for a while, or trying a different musical pursuit for a bit. I don't think there is anything wrong with any of that. Ultimately, keeping an open mind, being prepared to broaden your skill set, and being easy to work with, is the best thing you can do.

SS: How do you see the future for music? How do you see it for female musicians? Have you noticed any positive changes—or not?
ER: I think it is fairly impossible to comment on the future of music. Currently, I see a lot of positive change in many ways in terms of the general public being keen to engage with musicians and support music being made. Similarly, for female musicians, there is no way to know. One can only hope that as society in general improves and makes itself into a more accepting place and a place that places less emphasis on your gender and other factors out of your control that music will follow along with that. I have certainly noticed some positive changes. I have known older musicians who were in a mentoring role or high up in the education system, perhaps in universities, who are making a

conscious effort to see if they can keep track of and cater to the needs of all different students, not limited to gender, and that can only be a good thing. Personally, I think the only way we can make a lasting difference to diversity that we see in music circles is from the ground up, i.e., education systems making themselves not necessarily more welcoming but more available to all types of people—more outreach work within disadvantaged communities. That will lead to more young people coming up through music education systems—and not necessarily education systems but the general scene—and suddenly it will not be such a big deal to be a female musician. It will not be such a shock to anyone's system to see a woman playing the saxophone at a jazz gig. When we reach that point, I think that is ultimately successful because my personal aspiration is for when people mention me the word female need not come in front of the word saxophonist or musician. I am just a musician.

NATASHA SEALE

Photo Credit: Ross Powell

"I once heard musicians are mood shamans. A good analogy. Music unites people; it is the most powerful reminder of being human."

I first heard Natasha when I reviewed one of her albums. Then I saw her perform at Crazy Coqs, where she got the attention of a lively audience. She told wonderful stories between each song; one memorable one was of how she was in a West End show and a guy kept talking to her (slightly annoying). She had very large speakers she took to gigs and he offered to store them and bring them to every gig—which he did for some time, and every time he would speak to her (slightly annoying). The upshot to all this was the guy was now putting the children to bed as Natasha performed—a story that got the audience laughing and very much on Natasha's side.

It is difficult to pick highlights out from Natasha's career to date because there have been so many, from West End shows like Les Misérables, *to packing venues including Pizza Express, Crazy Coqs, and the 606 Club in London or performing with Alfie Bo at the Royal Variety Show or appearing in shows like* Aspects of Love *and* Mamma Mia *or playing Despina in Glyndebourne's hip hop opera* School 4 Lovers*, to name a very few. Natasha is at home singing or acting, usually combining both.*

SS: Can you tell me how you came to perform music?

NS: My Welsh mum had scholarships to Rome and Vienna as a young opera singer from a working-class background. Her dad worked at Cefn Coed Colliery, and my granny at the nursing hospital nearby. Mum studied further at Trinity and the Royal College of Music working as an opera singer for a while in London, before having me and my sister. Like all new mums, she diversified, focusing on pianist and repetiteur work. And she had a lovely children's choir. Music everywhere! Dad loved the romantic operas—super loud—Maria Callas, Joan Sutherland, and Sarah Vaughan. We sang in the church choir every week. I used to come up with alternative harmonies; they were far more satisfying intervals than the ones we were supposed to learn (I thought this became a bit of a theme for me)! My sister and I were made to sing whenever the opportunity arose (which was often) in front of Mum's friends, part of this concert, or for that occasion. We were super shy and very reluctant to accommodate, especially after our parents divorced. To "perform" on demand was not good for us, looking back. We began with violin lessons; my sister had Suzuki lessons—can't remember why I didn't have them too. But I longed to! I went to all her Suzuki workshops and camps but sat on the sidelines, observing with my violin. Regrettably, I moved away from piano as well after a few years (not before discovering a "tarantella," which completely swept me away)! With clarinet, we were getting closer to a profound satisfaction, enjoying many experiences of the county youth orchestra, and I stuck with it (although I still wanted to do my alternative harmonic endings). One afternoon, there was a trip with the school choir to the Albert Hall to sing Orff's *Carmina Burana*. There was a huge orchestra and loads of other schools. The opening, those dramatic drums, our voices in unison. I had a totally visceral experience—a big epiphany in that moment. The human voice holds the greatest self-expression—or rather I found the instrument that held the most freedom and relief, for me, was singing. I'd had elocution lessons to counteract the shyness and build confidence so the spoken word alone, too, held great catharsis for me—bingo! What a revelation. And of course, you think everyone else can sing the same as you.

Music competition festivals for my mum with me were just disappointing. I wasn't comfortable with classical singing like she was. I liked pop songs. I wanted to back-phrase and slur the notes (no change there). My dad took me to Jenny Miller, an opera singer, where I gained real insight with breathing, I got it. But I wanted to sing Whitney Houston's songs, not Mozart. Gigging in wine bars in a duo led to more residencies, singing soul, American Songbook and contemporary classics. I went to the US, met more jazzers in the Rocky Mountains, gigging in Breckenridge, Keystone, and Vale. It was then I realized that I might be quite good at singing. While in the US I sent an audition tape. I already had a place at London's Mountview but sent one to Liverpool Institute for Performing Arts. The facilities meant being torn to study either acting or songwriting, which was okay there. I was still oscillating between singing and the spoken word, never quite fully committing to one, for the love and need of the other! So, while on the acting degree I joined a few serious music students and jazzers. We formed a new band, Morwenna, my middle name, and we had a few residencies in Liverpool. We once sailed across the water, invited to perform in the Isle of Man Jazz Festival. We were the youngest band there. Jazz music was intoxicating! I loved the culture around it, the freedom, the improvisation, the communication, dedication, and respect for the music and the lineage of giants.

After signing with my first agent, before graduating, I would pop down to London from Liverpool for auditions. Just before permanently moving down, I was asked to sing solo with the Liverpool Philharmonic Orchestra and Choir at the Philharmonic Hall for a world premiere of *Red Ribbon Requiem* in Latin! It was a great confidence boost. Now living in London, I'd regularly appear in café/piano bars and restaurants in the West End, and my favorite, the National Theatre Foyer with my trio. Whatever show you were in, you sing it into your muscles, I was always acutely aware of this and on the lookout to sing other styles at every opportunity. I studied with Mary Hammond for a small stretch and a lot of different musical directors. I wrote with a few too. I feel most of my knowledge around singing is from great artists and practitioners: Donna Soto-Morettini, Liane Carroll, Sara Coleman, and Claire Martin.

SS: Do you play other instruments?
NS: Piano, ukulele, (accompaniment only), clarinet, and very recently a baritone horn. My kids play the cornet, and I want to hang out with them, so we've all joined the local wind band. I love it.

SS: What genres do you play—how do they differ/make you feel? Do you have a favorite?

NS: Vocal jazz/blues/folk is the closest to the natural speech register and my center. So, this is the more natural "go-to" when writing songs and connecting feelings from my inner world to fragments of rhythm or melody. I begin at the piano, starting with speech. This is where I loiter most, genre-wise. Here is where your truth is, I believe. I don't like to get caught up in genre. Stylistically I'm very versatile and hang out in the zone the instrumentation dictates, whatever this may be.

As vocal jazz/blues is not heightened like musical theater or operetta, in fact, quite the opposite, it's a more accessible way into my songwriting. Nowadays, the more grounded and comfortable I am in my skin, I want to spend more time in vocal jazz/blues and less time in other genres. I adore how swing jazz and Latin jazz feels—the energy and freedom in it! It makes me feel joyous and completely energized, so this is a favorite, I think. Having said this, it depends on your mood, right? Blues accesses my pathos—which I have plenty of! Soul and R&B, a soulful riff connects me to a more sassy, sensual physicality—also part of me.

When I crave vital catharsis, when the stakes are high, it's music theater or a power pop ballad. The difference being effort levels and the belt—the money note. I am very comfortable here too because sometimes such heightened emotion is required, i.e., when trying to process big or difficult feelings. It's alchemy—deepening your connection to the emotion—like building a bridge from the music to yourself; it really helps. (This is interesting for me to write as I've just realized why I'm reluctant to put ballads into my set lists!) I also love how empowering and powerful the community is in singing choral/ensemble a cappella and gospel. This is what we all missed in the pandemic—the unison of human voices together.

SS: As a female, have you ever felt treated differently as a musician than if you were male? If so, can you tell me how and whether you were able to do anything about this?

NS: All the time! Half an hour ago! Is it that I'm female, or a singer, or a combination of these? Or is it that I'm a Hastings girl with Welsh wanderings? Who knows? I'm educated and my working-class roots proudly pop.

I've been told by someone supportive in the industry that there are "so many singer-songwriters out there. It's saturated, it's too difficult these days."

(Like it's a choice?) It was a more welcoming situation, however, for my male counterpart at the time. The longer you are in this game, the swifter you become at recognizing the truth. It's important, I believe, to surround yourself with people who like your thing and move swiftly onward if your instinct tells you otherwise. Several years back I was dropped by my agent—a chap—when I disclosed my pregnancy to him. Because he "knew how this would roll out." A previous client had apparently said she was ready to go back to work and in fact wasn't (therefore I was going to do the same, of course). I'm not sure he would have got away with that now! I'm cross with myself that I accepted his ignorance—it was my first baby. Nowadays, my skin is thicker, and I like to think I'm wiser. Navigating this industry remains challenging on many levels, pretty much every step of the way, I've found this many times with males and on occasion with females. However, band leading and collaborating in the world of jazz is where I have grown most as an artist. It's where I continue to learn difficult and rewarding lessons—not least being economical with my language and vocabulary while on and off the stand! And to forgo the high heels and dress—although I won't be giving up the rouge lips anytime soon.

SS: Have you ever come across bullying or been bullied in your career as a musician? If so, can you explain this and how it made you feel?
NS: Unfortunately, yes, probably more times than I care to remember—and I think I'm fairly strong. It is an attempt to disempower you, and that's not kind or nice and can feel very isolating and deeply disappointing, especially when you naturally have an optimistic outlook. Intimidation—sexual or otherwise—controlling, bamboozling, gatekeeping, passive aggression, and withholding behaviors in any capacity, are all unacceptable. Yet I do believe it's universal, it's in all industries, some more than others. We're talking about power struggles. So where does this stem from? A happy, fulfilled place?—nope! And it is exactly this premise that helps me navigate the vicissitudes of both my career and my personal life. It's their problem, not mine. The only way to deal with it is to say it out loud, preferably to someone, and change our behavior—the way we react in response to it. Although the most difficult part is recognizing it, calling it what it is (and as soon as possible). This is the hard bit—even today. However it is dressed up/veiled, paying attention to your gut is paramount. If you are at the receiving end of some kind of behavior this can be incredibly confusing and disappointing. Often (the inner dialogue) goes like this: "Did that actually just happen; did they actually just say that? Why did they say/do

that?" Because it is often so unexpected, certainly from a colleague or industry professional, whom you respect, it takes time to assimilate—and this is the problem, for me, the gap that takes place after the moment has passed, yet before it is processed. Not responding at that moment is a missed opportunity, which means it can/will happen again until you give a firm boundary.

I know when I wasn't married to a firefighter, encountering toxic, inappropriate, and unprofessional behavior was more frequent. But, yes, it does still happen—someone just trying their luck and underestimating your emotional and innate intelligence presuming you're not savvy or bold enough to challenge. I have better tools now. Trust your gut.

SS: What experiences in music have made you grow as a musician? Were there events that happened which had a profound effect on you?
NS: I emphasized collaborative environments and experiences. I had resident stints at Snape Maltings as a performer for Jerwood Opera Writing Foundation, which changed my life. I felt so lucky to be in a close and beautiful environment, witnessing and being part of the creative process from conception to performance; it blew my mind! Daily workshops, living, working, and creating with artists, poets, composers, playwrights, librettists, instrumentalists, videographers, designers, and directors, all exchanging ideas, it was a dream to behold. I remember Sir Harrison Burtwhistle telling me to not be overly concerned with "the dots—my instinct was correct." Each time this was a deeply creative, transformative, and informing process—such a gift.

Sitzprobe (a process where singers sit in the orchestra to help blend with the musicians) with a full orchestra is overwhelming at the best of times. Back in the day when *Les Misérables* had nearly thirty orchestra members, this was very emotional. It was incredibly memorable as my first West End show, but I'll never forget our sitzprobe (a seated rehearsal for orchestra and singers) with the Southbank Sinfonia for Glyndebourne's first hip hopera, *School 4 Lovers*. This was a profoundly transformative moment—where Mozart meets hip hop (!), I was swept away on Mozart's swells of the orchestra and the collision of these two art forms so familiar to me. The tension and parallels from these two contrasting worlds, up until that time, I was comfortable in—separately. They were never meant to meet! I think I'd compartmentalized the music. Opera represented "home life (my parents)" and hip hop a shift toward a new home (my gang), my deep rebellion after my parents divorced, as a teen in Hastings, full of the sounds of ragga, dancehall, reggae, house, the genesis of hip hop. This combination was indirectly giving the gift of processing a difficult childhood and more. It was truly exhilarating. The challenges—the sextet! We traveled to Estonia and Finland playing in opera houses. Rehearsing, devising, and collectively creating at Glyndebourne, in that incredible space, was also truly memorable.

I found my voice really when I took on a huge learning curve when my eldest child went to nursery. I completed a long-distance masters in Songwriting, with several residencies at Bath Spa. This was a beautiful time of collaboration too, entering the world of singer-songwriters. I enjoyed it immensely. The culmination was the release of my debut album, *A Bigger Sky*, essentially the final project. I had all these songs that I wanted to put out into the world, and I did. I wrote and produced them solo. It was enlightening scheduling, collaborating, arranging, and booking musicians and studios. It was distributed by the 33Jazz Records label, and I launched the album with my quartet at the Stables, Wavendon. The gig was days before the Grenfell fire. I'd written a song about the London Fire Brigade, the difficult job they do, and how we need them (I'm married to an LFB firefighter). I squeezed the song in, wanted to try it out and see what the response was, and we performed it to a very appreciative audience that night.

We launched *A Bigger Sky* with a set at Cheltenham Jazz Festival too. This was six months after the birth of my second child. (I remember breast pumping just before walking on stage.) Wow! I'd never performed at a festival before—how empowering. The sun was going down and there I was, singing a song I'd written! "Earth Flower" was played beautifully by my musicians to a crowd of happy people enjoying the music with my two little earth flowers, their cheeky faces in the audience. It doesn't get better than that. Although, later that evening, we were playing to the VIP room and Giles Peterson—in fact, lots of music and radio industry people were present—and instead of hanging out after, all I could think about was running back to that hotel room to feed my baby.

The most profound all-time learning has got to be becoming a bandleader for my one-woman projects. I had to step up. I'd been to several game-changing workshops with mentors and amazing musicians Liane Carroll, Sara Coleman, and Sophie Bancroft, and all this learning needed to be put into practice. I'm lucky enough to have a great double bass player, Rob Rickenberg, whom I've learned so much from over the years, he's a great teacher and great with people. I wanted to adopt his ways on the stand with the chaps! I went to see Claire Martin, who inspired me to create a show around one of my icons, Rosemary Clooney. After researching Clooney's interesting life, reading loads of books, creating a verbatim script, and picking the songs and my favorite arrangements, the result was a transformative tour. I feel like I've learned in abundance. So much so that I went in for another! I wrote a show around bandleader Duke Ellington, titled *Universal Ellington*, once again encouraged by Claire, only this time with arrangements, a whole level up. The learning on this tour has been accelerated and I feel like I've found my voice. My forthcoming one-woman show will be entirely my own material, my own script, and stories, working alongside an arranger who will enhance the songs, using very different voices, and new instrumentation to me. All those bits of manuscript, tunes, notebooks, and diaries coming together. It feels exciting.

SS: Who inspires you? Not just musicians perhaps, but anyone, and can you explain how they inspire you and why?
NS: My children. The way they experience nature, their relationship and respect toward all living beings, and their unconditional love. Each day you clock their wonder, energy, and joy and you marvel at it and, of course, the opposite (my God, the drama as well, when we can't find a book or a shoe, unable to get out of the house, always, always late). And the down stuff too around parenting when they are encountering their own challenges and you can't fix it. This is a constant source of inspiration. My response to these little people.

It's crucial to me my children are connected to the inspiration of nature, music, and books, as I am in this tech-heavy, AI world. I had a challenging childhood, which dissipated with music and stories and being in nature's nourishing growth. We strongly believe connecting with nature is connecting to the present moment, to yourself; nothing beats this.

I am inspired by anyone who creates and brings people together, empowering them via arts and music, whether it is creating paintings, music, or dance. There are too many individuals, groups, and organizations to mention, and I eternally add to the list. So, let's say all the good eggs out there. Top of the list is Shakespeare: we can still learn a lot from his timeless insights into human nature, and his way with words is still completely relevant. Jess Phillips MP because she's a legend. David Attenborough is an incredible human—I think most will agree. Tim Minchin, for giving the modern world the lyrics and music to *Matilda*, a gift of empowerment to generations of children, and Jacob Collier—a truly collaborative spirit and beyond, transforming his audiences all over the world into a massive choir… so much to come from him. I realize there's space here still for working-class female writers—maybe I'll fill that. I'm deeply inspired by people who question, raise their heads above the parapet, and use their platform for their voice. Also, I am very inspired by my husband and his anchoring pragmatism. And the fact he's not on any social media and never will be. So cool.

SS: If you had to explain, what would you say music did for/to you? Is there some part it taps into?
NS: To add to what I said earlier, music unites people and strongly encourages people to commune, connect, and recognize themselves in others. It cleanses and makes you engage with an array of emotions, joy, sadness, nostalgia, etc.

SS: Could it ever be just a job?
NS: No. There is nothing as immediate and visceral as music—we know its power. It can transport you immediately to your younger self. Photographs can do this also, but music is more three-dimensional and immersive.

I once heard musicians are mood shamans. A good analogy. Music unites people; it is the most powerful reminder of being human.

SS: What would you say to an aspiring female musician?
NS: Learn an instrument or two, seek out your tribe, only work with people who get your thing and want to support it, and find your female mentors and your confidantes. Be prepared to educate (why wouldn't you want to do this?). Pick a partner who understands the world you invest so fully in—ideally not someone so far removed from it. No, it doesn't need to be a bass or piano player! Don't strive for the ideal of work/life balance. There is no such thing. It is about your autonomy and making the right choices for you and your family at that time.

Eat, sleep, take vitamins, and trust your gut.

SS: Would you recommend music as a way to make a living?
NS: Yes. It is a gift and a privilege. It is challenging. Part and parcel of being a musician involves freelancing as an educator/facilitator and any work that informs you as an artist, whatever that may be during a snowy February or on a sunny day in August. Some of the most interesting musicians/performers build their character between contracts. Sometimes you've got to go pull a

pint, wait tables, or work in a cinema—that's okay, because you learn equally valuable tools, not least how to interact with the general public, patter/banter. Ultimately what we do is communicate, building these skills is paramount... Then you're the brilliant person who sets up the very popular live music night. You just make it work.

SS: What characteristics do you need?
NS: To be open and honest, a whole lot of self-belief and determination, a great sense of humor, tough skin, and computer skills!

SS: If you had to explain the one thing (or more) you found which makes music worthwhile, what would this be?
NS: Connection, empowerment, freedom, hope/anticipation, alignment, peace, deep joy. The list is endless.

SS: Do you think the pandemic changed music and how we access it? Or do you think music and how we access it changes over time in any case?
NS: I think, whatever times we live in, music transcends, space, time, and language and continually metamorphoses. We relied on the arts heavily to get us through the pandemic. And live performance was sorely missed—fact. My belief is the more we move into this digital space, toward an atomized society, the greater the force is to commune with one another and with nature. You only have to look at the stats around festivals for this. We want musical experiences together and in nature. It's who we are. No amount of tech will change this, especially simulating a synthetic experience. We want/yearn/need the real resonant experience live music brings whether we are conscious of this or not.

SS: Is it possible to make a decent living as a musician? What would you advise to do this? What strengths do you need? Do you need a business plan, or to get a good manager? What makes the difference between aspiring, struggling, and being a success?
NS: Not necessary, but get business savvy. I guess it depends on the individual; certainly, it helps when someone can do the admin/graphics, the booking, and the chasing. When I'm overwhelmed, I always think how wonderful it would be to have a team managing your bookings and social media... And the payoff would be your autonomy. I struggle with this—control of my content/

opinions, etc. I am an artist as well, and I've studied and worked in other arts areas. If you are pedantic about language/imagery/color—I'm very picky about words and phrases, having someone else pretend they are you—how does that work? I do know myself better than anyone—and equally, I can put makeup on me better than anyone else!

(We have to engage with social media as musicians, but do we need to engage with social media's regular "feeds"? Thankfully algorithms have kyboshed "engaging" with feeds, no scrolling here now, which really works for me.)

Your strength is you, so to be you is super important. It sounds very clichéd, but I often get rebooked based upon the way I relate to audiences/promoters/programmers. It does work the other way too, though! Listen, you can be the most beautiful peach... You're not going to be everyone's cup of tea. Understanding this is freeing.

What makes the difference between aspiring, struggling, and being a success? This is entirely subjective. And certainly not measured in your following and your "likes." Success is different for everyone: my shoestring, low-budget, no-frills projects have been steeper learning curves, more valuable and fulfilling than shows with high-end production values, many times over. Having performed in a variety of venues from theaters above pubs to clubs to international arenas, crossing seas (and genres), it is typical to encounter pre-conceived notions (and great when you smash them away in performance). It is difficult for me to answer this question... What is the wider context? I always ask this. I've experienced much musical width and breadth, stylistically, with a focus on live performance. I've toured extensively and traveled to far-flung, interesting cities with work. This feels very lucky and successful. I feel like I have so many strings to my bow and will just keep on building and exploring these, which I find very exciting. I do feel very rich in terms of family and friends. You navigate according to your benchmark—not anyone else's. I'm not good at coasting. I like to challenge myself; this feels "aspiring" and "successful" at the same time to me. I seek out support from female mentors more experienced/knowledgeable than me, whom I wholeheartedly respect. Growing is crucial to me and feels successful too. Claire Martin is my go-to, and with her feedback, I'm good at creating projects that challenge. But you need that feedback to move forward and fill those missing gaps in knowledge.

SS: How do you see the future for music?

NS: Exciting and worrying. Live music and sharing space with people are so important, and my concern is that arts, culture, and music are devalued in education (and outside of it too in the demise of grassroots venues). Will tomorrow's talent slip through the cracks, especially in areas of the UK with less wealthy demographics? If a child can't access music lessons, a choir, or orchestra because of low funds or no funds—this will change the landscape dramatically... Is there also a bigger picture at stake here along the lines of undermining social cohesion? Post-pandemic, we all consciously now know how beneficial music is on many levels—it got us through lockdown. Ultimately, as musicians, we cannot ignore the music inside us. Therefore, I hope this means music and musicians will always find a way—as they have done for centuries.

SS: How do you see it for female musicians? Have you noticed any positive changes—or not?

NS: I see a slight shift, yes, but my goodness there's a way to go! Has the male gaze less gravitas these days? Possibly perhaps less than when I was growing up—I think this conversation is always worth unpacking, at every opportunity. Following #Metoo, the Keychange movement shone a terrific spotlight. But there is work to be done still, always. We need to keep the conversation going and the awareness up and keep questioning the fundamentals, gender parity, conscious bias, and focus on positive imagery for female musicians. (I do recognize an awareness with younger generations of female musicians breaking through regarding positive imagery.) Are female images greater or lesser than their equivalent? Are they sexualized or not? These things are so important. Do they teach it on your degree? Not always, or perhaps a more accurate answer is, not enough. Women in Jazz Media are a platform championing and celebrating phenomenal female jazz musicians with a strong awareness around identity. For me it's great to see "Mothers in Jazz"—at last! Visibility, breaking the culture of silence around parenting! PiPA (Parents in Performing Arts) with the "Best Practice Charter," "Balancing Act" and more recently "Bittersweet Symphony" within the classical music spheres are leaps forward; didn't have this when I was younger. We have to keep having conversations because it foregrounds what we do. Aligning with organizations like these is a pretty important and prudent move. Baby steps.

BRIGITTE BERAHA

Photo Credit: Rolf Schoellkopf

"There is such beautiful music being made and played right now. As an improvising musician, it isn't always easy to make money from this music, but we persist. I think the future for female musicians is looking brighter today. I am seeing more and more wonderful female musicians coming out of colleges, which is exciting to witness and will help re-address the gender balance organically."

Improvising vocalist, composer and lyricist Brigitte Beraha was born in Milan to a Turkish father and a Turkish-British mother Her multinational, multilingual, and musical upbringing led Brigitte to embrace many influences and genres, from jazz and Latin to classical and electronic. Brigitte has worked with a wide range of musicians and recorded several critically acclaimed albums. She has toured Europe and the UK. She was nominated for the coveted Jazz FM Vocalist of the Year Award in 2022.

SS: Can you tell me how you came to play music and how you found the instrument you specialize in? Do you play other instruments?

BB: We had a piano at home that my dad played—back in Istanbul, he used to play for a Turkish pop star, Erol Buyikburc in the sixties, and what was left from that was him occasionally entertaining us with his raucous voice and piano playing; I used to love listening to him even though he was doing it more for comedy value than anything else. I would then spend hours messing around on the piano and working out songs by Elton John, Jacques Brel, the Beatles and Dire Straits. I didn't have any formal training, but playing and singing were always part of my life. I used to know the entirety of *La traviata*, which had been given to me in CD format, so I would sing along to Pavarotti and Sutherland and drive my family crazy. I loved listening to classical music, but also pop and French chanson, and anything I could get my hands and ears on. I eventually had some piano lessons as a teenager, which I loved. I remember my piano teacher saying I was gifted, but it was a shame I started so late, too late. I never even thought a career in music was possible. It wasn't until I moved to London at nineteen that I started to pursue music. I enrolled in a specialist music A level course as a piano player. I also sang in the choir and with my newly found musician friends. It wasn't until my second year at Goldsmiths College that I switched to voice; it was clear people seemed to enjoy my singing more than my piano playing!

SS: What genres do you play—how do they differ/make you feel? Do you have a favorite genre and why?

BB: I play mainly jazz and improvised music. At Kingsway College (the Music A level course) I met some friends who were really into jazz, so that was the real beginning of my passion for jazz. Before that, as a classical piano player, I used to get terrible stage fright and would occasionally forget what came next in the piece or it would be a terrible thing to play a wrong note within a Chopin waltz, I couldn't deal with it. Suddenly, singing jazz, these fears were gone and replaced by new challenges. I instantly felt more at home with it, it was fun, and I found this new freedom in music that wasn't there before.

I love interpreting jazz and Latin standards, as well as more contemporary repertoire, including original material. I have recently ventured into more experimental and electronic territories; I've always loved electronic and classical music but have kept the genres compartmentalized in my head, until I realized they didn't have to be.

With various projects (such as Eddie Parker's Debussy Mirrored Ensemble or Babelfish), I also started delving into cross-genres, i.e., bringing in classical or folk music within the jazz and improvisatory mediums. I love the exploration, freedom of expression and interaction that all this music and musicians help generate. It's what makes me happy. I don't favor any genre; it is the beauty of the material per se and what we do with it which is exciting.

SS: As a female, have you ever felt treated differently as a musician than if you were male?
BB: No, I've never felt treated differently as a female. I have rarely had any bad experiences, not in a musical context anyway. I would say I have felt more of a stigma with being a vocalist, with often the assumption that if I am a singer, I am not a musician, and having to prove myself a little more than if I had been an instrumentalist. It is generally okay, though, and I think people are becoming more educated: I am now seeing less of the frustrating "singers and musicians" notices and more "singers and instrumentalists welcome," which is somewhat encouraging.

SS: Have you ever come across bullying or been bullied in your career as a musician? If so, can you explain this and how it made you feel?
BB: Yes, I have seen bullying occur in my career, as I have seen it happen in everyday life. In my experience, bullying has come from people who might have a sense of entitlement (i.e., have been doing this for longer), have been educated badly, have had difficult life experiences themselves, or have been mentally unstable generally. My aim is always to try and be as compassionate as possible. However, if it ends up affecting me and my peers, I will usually call it out or/and refuse to work with the bully in question in the future. It's not worth it! Playing music should ideally be joyous, and we should all be treated with respect and respect each other as human beings, wherever we are in our musical journey.

SS: What experiences in music have made you grow as a musician? Were there events that happened which had a profound effect on you?
BB: I think listening to loads of amazing music on my own and with others when growing up has had a deep impact. I also learned so much behind the piano on my own as a child, spending many solitary hours practicing and singing without really knowing what I was doing. Later on, watching my peers and musical heroes do their thing and getting to play with them, i.e., going to

Ronnie Scott's every night to watch Airto Moreira and Flora Purim when I first came to London. So many new musical experiences that have helped shape me, starting at Kingsway College and meeting gifted tutors and musicians there, the Glamorgan summer school, spending a year at GSMD (Guildhall School of Music & Drama) and meeting all my brilliant tutors and peers, many of whom I'm still friends with today, getting to sing the "Sweet Time Suite" with Kenny Wheeler—I remember being both extremely nervous but incredibly elated—that was the most amazing experience ever. Somehow, I knew that whatever musical situation I would be thrown in after that, I should be okay.

SS: Who inspires you? Not just musicians perhaps, but anyone, and can you explain how they inspire you and why?
BB: Honestly, I get inspired by my friends and close ones every day, but also by everything around me, not just people. I get inspired by nature and its tenacity.

SS: If you had to explain, what would you say music did for/to you? Is there some part it taps into? Does it make you feel emotional? Could it ever be just a job?
BB: For me, music is a great companion. Growing up, I would sometimes cry when listening to it, or it would unleash so much joy, excitement, or wonder; it always managed to hit the right nerve and provoke intense reactions. Nowadays, I know the more I try to analyze music, though enriching in itself, the less emotional I get; so, I purposefully often close up the analytical side of my brain to allow myself to "feel" more, whatever the music or the feeling might be. Music has a way of accessing certain states of being that nothing else can. Could it ever be just a job? Yes, I think it can be just a job, but these days I feel very lucky that most of the music I perform I love or feel happy to be invested in and lose myself in.

SS: What would you say to an aspiring female musician? Would you recommend music as a way to make a living? What characteristics do you need?
BB: I know it can feel tough for some female musicians to feel integrated. I would say that I have never thought about gender differentiation as a musician, I have always looked at making music with humans regardless of their gender. I think that if—on a personal and individual level—we make it an issue, then it can become an issue when it's possible it was never there in the first place. It's about sticking with the nice people and those whom we feel a strong musical connection with, regardless of race or gender.

If you know you can't live without music, then trust your instincts. Don't force things, see where they take you but be strong within yourself. Take constructive criticism (I am so thankful for it!) but don't let people put you down or tell you what to do. Ideally, have a mentor who can help guide you. Everyone will have an opinion, but it might not necessarily be the right one for you musically. Listen, interact, but make your own choices. I would definitely recommend music as a way of living if it is right for you! It's been right for me, though music can entail many things, and, in my case, to make a living, I try and balance my working life between performing, writing, and teaching music. This way currently works for me because I have found a way of loving it and enjoying the ride, through its inevitable ups and downs. If I stopped enjoying it, I would have to rethink.

SS: If you had to explain the one thing (or more) you found which makes music worthwhile, what would this be?
BB: Playing music with and for others is very special; that moment when we all connect through the magical unfolding of sound, that's quite something. Even if our perceptions and reactions might be different, we all spent a moment in time sharing the same sonic universe.

SS: Do you think the pandemic changed music and how we access it? Or do you think music and how we access it changes over time in any case?
BB: This is a tricky one, as I think it'll take some more time before the whole impact of the pandemic is understood. There are so many strands to that question. I am sure many albums—like my solo album *By the Cobbled Path* (2021)—would have been different or even not existed without the pandemic.

I think it has changed the state of music for many people, both performers and concertgoers. I have noticed both performers and concertgoers seemed to be so much more elated going to performances right after the pandemic, a reminder to not take live music for granted.

People have reacted differently to music life after the pandemic. Some people have become more cautious about going out to gigs or booking at the last minute, which makes it difficult for venues and musicians. I am aware of some musicians being very busy before the pandemic and not so after. It has certainly shaken the order of things. Music seems to be more appreciated online or in little snippets on social media these days, though I'm not sure this can be blamed on the pandemic.

More livestreamed events are a positive outcome of the pandemic, especially for those who are less mobile or unable to go out to see a live gig in person but can still share the musical experience from the comfort of their own home.

SS: Thinking of that young aspiring musician, do you think it is possible to make a decent living as a musician? How would you advise her to do this and what might her strengths need to be? Does she need to be a businessperson, to plan, and get a good manager? What makes the difference between aspiring, struggling, and being a success?
BB: I think it does help to get a clear idea of what success means to you. Is it making loads of money, is it contentment, enjoying what one does, etc.? Having some clarity in that respect will certainly help toward knowing if your goals are achievable and which direction to take.

From a young age, I knew I didn't want to feel ruled by money—so, while I knew I wasn't striving to be rich, I equally did not want to have to worry too much about money, but more importantly, I wanted to do something that I loved. When it became clear I would be a musician, in the beginning, I'd go flyering, stewarding, giving French lessons, singing lessons, doing functions, and solo piano/voice bar gigs, etc. I would look for work and say yes to pretty much everything. I didn't necessarily like it all, but it was my way of getting the ball rolling. Although at times I struggled, persistence allowed me to make it work for me and eventually achieve one of my goals, to love what I do. Make sure to work joyfully at honing your craft, don't just focus on the business side of things, and vice versa! I don't think I am so good at business unfortunately (I realize I should have spent a little more time on that side of things, though it's never too late). However, I was given good advice early on when I get offered work; often not enough info is given. Don't be afraid to ask for more detail, i.e., when, where, and how much? And don't feel bad about asking these things. This is our work. We are lucky to love it, but it is our work, and we should be paid for it.

If you are looking to do something artistic like making an album, planning properly, and making a timeline for it is always good! You want your music to be heard, so take your time in planning properly for it, and don't be afraid to ask around for advice from those who are a little ahead in their journey!

Re: getting management: toward the beginning of my musical life, someone did offer to manage me and find me gigs, but nothing really came of it, and I quickly understood that to get things happening I had to take care of them myself. That is my own experience though, and I've never had a manager since, so can't really advise on that. Again, talk to people around you to get more perspective, and see what is right for you! Of course, some luck and life events can also take a part. Be open to this but have your head screwed on!

SS: How do you see the future for music? How do you see it for female musicians? Have you noticed any positive changes—or not?
BB: It's so difficult to think about the future of music. The future can look a little gloomy sometimes, but I like to stay hopeful and concentrate on the now. There is such beautiful music being made and played right now. As an improvising musician, it isn't always easy to make money from this music, but we persist. I think the future for female musicians is looking brighter today. I am seeing more and more wonderful female musicians coming out of college, which is exciting to witness and will help re-address the gender balance organically.

I know a lot of people are working behind the scenes to help make this happen, which is great, but I am also wary of segregation (i.e., occasional all-girl bands for the sake of it) and imposing a fifty percent rule on female/male musicians at festivals, for example, when that ratio clearly isn't naturally there yet. What these "quick fixes" may do is give a platform to lesser able female musicians and counteract the good work that's being done. I'd hate to think that audiences will say, "See, men play better than women!" because some festival organizer has had to bring in fifty percent of female musicians to their festival regardless of musical quality. However, the positive from that is they just can't get away (or be lazy) with not booking any female musicians anymore! It just has to be done well to have the deserved positive impact.

I did however also notice I worked more during the "Jazz: International Women's Day" week. Maybe just a coincidence, but certainly I see some promoters still don't want to book two female saxophonists in a row when they have no qualms about booking three male saxophonists in a row. Be aware of equal opportunities—this is indeed very important!—AND book excellence, don't be lazy. But I am on the whole optimistic. In my world, gender isn't an issue. It so happens that my Lucid Dreamers band is fifty percent male and fifty percent female, but that was because I really wanted to play with George, Alcyona, and Tim! Hopefully we'll get to a point when this is the case across the board, and we won't even have to think about this anymore because it will just be happening organically.

JEANIE BARTON

Photo Credit: Luke Rayner

"There is no drug quite like that connection between the band and the audience. It is actual magic."

Jeanie Barton was a principal in the National Youth Music Theatre before studying with Anita Wardell. She studied jazz harmony at Morley College in London and sang and compered for Laurie Morgan's trio at their weekly event in North London. She has supported Georgie Fame, worked with Luddy Samms of The Drifters, and performed for Samuel L. Jackson, Shirley Bassey, and Pierce Brosnan. Jeanie was voted "Best Newcomer" at the Marlborough Jazz Festival 2015, and she has performed at some of the most respected venues. She is also a journalist, writing for London Jazz News and Nottingham Live.

SS: Can you tell me how you came to perform? Do you play other instruments?
JB: I started singing as a child, before I can even remember, along to the radio, etc. Strangely, I apparently seemed to know many songs without having heard

them before. My mum believes in inherited memory. I especially loved old musicals and in senior school got the chance to perform in many, which sent me on quite a path of performing in music theater shows and plays too. I was in the National Youth Music Theatre for many years and had good roles, then ended up working professionally in theater in and around London mostly. My parents met in a local drama group, and when they used to set up the set in the theater there was a piano there—I would sit and play on it for hours/days and quickly realized I had a knack for transcribing by ear. I used to play anything and everything. In my teens, my parents bought me an old piano and I continued this process of self-teaching. I had some lessons but found them frustrating, as it was like going backward in terms of the complexity of what I had taught myself, and I used to cheat, not reading the music but rather just copying by ear. I didn't get on with written music for this reason until I found jazz notation (chord charts depicting jazz harmony) in my twenties. Then I found I could both write down what I was playing and read music that way—I can read the stave but am slow.

SS: *What genres do you play, and do you have a favorite?*
JB: I especially love jazz because of the dense, complex harmonies—I love all emotive music. Finding Lambert, Hendricks & Ross in my twenties was an epiphany, as I was floored by their vocal harmonies, witty lyrics, scat singing, and so on. I also especially dig Latin music: Cuban, Brazilian, etc., exotic grooves and chromatic paths. I sing/perform a lot of these. I sing bebop classics too, and this is likely my preferred genre, but at the same time, I perform in other pop ensembles and do lots of pop numbers in a jazz style at my piano like Postmodern Jukebox. I'm a closet rapper too and once performed live and ended up rapping with an electro-swing outfit who remixed one of my songs. I would love to do more of that or work with hip hop artists one day!

SS: *As a female, have you ever felt treated differently as a musician than if you were male? If so, can you tell me how and whether you were able to do anything about this?*
JB: I can't say I have, although I guess I fit the mold of being a singer (girl singer is pretty standard). I think male colleagues are happy and sometimes surprised that I have good practical music knowledge though and that I play piano. I would not say I have felt demeaned in any way though; people in the jazz sphere tend to be very nice and down-to-earth. I don't find it as highly competitive and bitchy as music theater. Although I made many good friends there, it can

be a bit of a wasp's nest! I like that the jazz community feels encouraging and supportive of each other largely—there is less jealousy perhaps because there is more individuality, I think.

SS: Have you ever come across bullying or been bullied in your career as a musician?

JB: Once I had a tenor saxophonist try to hit me in the face while playing his horn as I offered my mic to him—he wasn't well though and was in and out of mental institutions, so I didn't take his aggression personally, but it shook me up.

SS: What experiences in music have made you grow as a musician? Were there events that happened that had a profound effect on you?

JB: I compered and sang with Laurie Morgan's trio most Sundays for more than a decade—he was a drummer and vibes player and a founder of bebop in Britain. I learned so much from those old guys who were exceptional musicians yet so down-to-earth and kind—they have all sadly died now but I treasure the memory of them and being embraced by their band. A few years back I played a function with Tony Kofi on sax, Cliff Brown on bass, and Ian Beestin on drums. Ian had organized the gig and I was worried beforehand as there was no harmonic instrument in the line-up, but it was a liberating experience we are going to repeat soon. We all just seemed to click and weave in and out of each other so well creating musical shapes with the space; it was thrilling.

SS: Who inspires you? Can you explain how they inspire you and why?

JB: Vocally, as a child, I was fascinated by Doris Day and Vera Lynn—their purity of tone and vocal strength/accuracy—I learned to sing by mimicking them mostly. Once I became aware of jazz I listened to a lot of Ella's live recordings and learned her scats, also Carmen MacRae, Sarah Vaughan, Lambert, Hendricks & Ross, and Anita O'Day—and I binged on lots of instrumental bebop, Charlie Parker et al. Laurie Morgan was a valuable mentor to me, my "jazz dad" I called him. He and his family took care of me when my dad died in 2004. He was assistant musical director at the National Theatre when Lawrence Olivier was in charge and had so many stories and anecdotes. The friends and colleagues I met at his jam Downstairs at the King's Head in Crouch End all became like family to me, and although I now live in Nottingham, I get down as often as I can with my son to see them (those who are still with us and the new faces that come through). I met my late husband there too, so that club changed my life in every way. They all inspire me, as do my colleagues up here. They help me enjoy what I do and take risks. I don't have massive ambition. I'm quite content just making music and any small positivity I can give in any aspect of my life.

SS: If you had to explain, what would you say music did for/to you? Could it ever be just a job?
JB: It's a privilege to make money doing what I love. Yes, of course, it's all emotional—as my dad used to say, "Our well is near the top!" I feel like music is connection, access to a higher power, I don't know—I guess I'm a hippy, but I feel I'm wired up in such a way that I just can't help but make music and share it—I feel I receive through it too and find collaboration most fulfilling.

SS: What would you advise an aspiring female musician? Would you recommend music as a way to make a living? What characteristics do you need?
JB: I would not recommend to anyone of any gender music as a way to make a living—if money is what motivates you, go into banking or something! But I think if you can be reliable and professional as well as creative and passionate, you can earn a living in music—it's certainly not easy. The most talented are rarely reliable or organized enough to make a successful career financially from it. I don't think you should go into music for fame either. External considerations like money, power, or fame are at odds with the essence of creating/emoting. I would say to women and all genders there is no substitute for technical knowledge and practice when it comes to whatever instrument you aspire to play—enjoy your study and put your own personality/identity into what you do. This will earn respect from colleagues/promoters et al and set you apart.

SS: If you had to explain what makes music worthwhile, what would this be?
JB: The energy exchange of live performance. There is no drug quite like that connection between the band and the audience. It is actual magic. Recording is very different, but rewarding, as the live experiences are so fleeting. Teaching too, which I am doing more of, is satisfying—it's more sharing really, and to see someone improving and feeling pleased with themselves is a real boost.

SS: Do you think the pandemic changed music and how we access it? Or do you think music and how we access it changes over time in any case?
JB: Technology is a blessing and a curse. Even before the pandemic, digitization

133

reduced the value of recorded music to near zero—it's disgraceful. I think a lack of live music during the pandemic made people realize its value perhaps more. However, the economic fall-out means that it's another race to the bottom in terms of wages sadly (like after the 2007 crash). Live music is seen as a luxury item and one of the things first squeezed, unfortunately.

SS: Thinking of a young aspiring musician, how would you advise her and what might her strengths need to be? Does she need to be a businessperson, to plan, and get a good manager?
JB: Luck. But we can make our own luck by being persistent and professional. I suffered a lot of rejection and am not emotionally well equipped to deal with it, but I have learned with age that you have to bloody toughen up and keep on keeping on. Pick yourself up, dust yourself off, and start all over again! I'd like a manager and a PA, lol.

SS: How do you see the future of music? How do you see it for female musicians? Have you noticed any positive changes—or not?
JB: I think like with women's football, plus other female achievers, hopefully women musicians are becoming more visible and that can only help those up and coming. I hope I am a good example and that this interview helps to inspire you!

RACHEL SUTTON

Photo Credit: Polly Hancock

"One thing I've noticed that's changing is there is more of an openness about being a mother in the music industry. And about time too."

Songwriter, lyricist, and performer, Rachel Sutton has worked with some of music's notable performers, including Liane Carroll, Lance Ellington, and more. She has worked as an actress, and her background in theater is brought to her performances as she combines her love of lyrics with her love of swing music. A graduate of Glamorgan University and the Welsh College of Music and Drama, Rachel toured Europe in plays and then award-winning shows at Edinburgh and New York's Fringe festivals. This experience led her to sing full-time as her career. Rachel has sold out venues, and her role in Lansky: The Mob's Money Man *at the Queen Elizabeth Hall, Southbank, and Cadogan Hall received wide acclaim.*

SS: Can you tell me how you came to play music and how you found the instrument you specialize in? Do you play other instruments?
RS: I have always been a performer. Although I started as an actor, after a few years I found myself leaning more toward singing, not just because I was having more success with it, but also because I loved the interplay of lyrics, music, and communication. For me, singing is still acting but it's just done in a different way. I like to create characters and scenarios in my head when I'm thinking about how to perform a song; the interpretation is unique to each singer and the receiving of it is unique to each listener. At one point, I was fortunate enough to be surrounded by lots of musicians who became friends and colleagues and from whom I received amazing support and encouragement—that was probably the catalyst for me becoming a professional singer. When I was a child, I remember long, luxurious days when I closed the curtains and turned the sitting room into a nightclub. I'd listen to my mother's wonderful records and imagine myself as a singer. So, as you can see, this need to perform has been going on for a long time! In terms of other instruments, I use the piano to write my music, but I wouldn't dream of saying I can play it properly.

SS: What genres do you play—how do they differ/make you feel? Do you have a favorite genre and why?
RS: My tastes have always been eclectic, so I wouldn't say I have a favorite genre. I found from quite a young age that my voice lent itself more naturally toward jazz, and my mother was a huge jazz fan, so I was lucky enough to have a whole host of beautiful records to listen to when I was growing up. And I think jazz lyrics are some of the best in the world—full of wit and joy and gentleness, too. I've found myself recently wanting to experiment more by pulling elements of folk into my songwriting. I find folk music incredibly moving and wistful and feel deeply connected on a level that's hard to describe when I hear it. And I love taking a contemporary piece and jazzing it up a bit! Music is about feelings, so I'll go with whatever speaks to me.

SS: As a female, have you ever felt treated differently as a musician than if you were male? If so, can you tell me how and whether you were able to do anything about this?

RS: There have certainly been a handful of occasions (luckily not many) where I think I've been treated differently because I'm a woman. I've been spoken to in ways that I definitely wouldn't have been if I was a man. And, at a certain point in my career, I've been spoken down to because I was less experienced than those around me. I think it's easy to go from zero to outrage in thirty seconds if you feel you are being undermined, but it's not the way forward. It's important to take a breath and think about what you need or want out of this situation you're in. It's so hard, I don't have the answers, but maintaining your composure and being very clear about what you'd like to happen is important.

SS: Have you ever come across bullying or been bullied in your career as a musician? If so, can you explain this and how it made you feel

RS: I'm so lucky to have never had this experience but I really feel for people who have. It is unacceptable and cruel. Always ask for help if this happens.

SS: What experiences in music have made you grow as a musician? Were there events that happened which had a profound effect on you?

RS: I married a musician! That helped a lot—haha! I've often berated myself for being a late developer. But it is what it is. I don't think I could write the music I do now or perform the way I do now if I was younger. That's not the way it is for everyone, but that's how my journey has been. Once you realize how complicated life can be and how untidy it is, that's one of the keys, I think. There's also something very tender about watching your parents grow old and finally understanding so much of what they went through when they were the age you are now! There's a lot of complexity and richness in that. Things become clearer—not always, of course! Losing my mother was one of the hardest things I ever had to go through, and I think something shifted in me at that moment, too. The song "A Million Conversations" is about that time, and it just poured out of me after Mum died. And I wanted it to be a universal song of grief so that others would understand and identify when they heard it—I hope I achieved that. In other ways, when you spend your life with a musician, as I do, you learn so much from them, and each day is about music in some form or another. I feel very lucky to have learned so much from my husband, Roland Perrin. I have a huge amount to thank him for.

SS: Who inspires you? Not just musicians perhaps, but anyone, and can you explain how they inspire you and why?

RS: There are so many people who inspire me, both in the music world and outside of it. Sometimes inspiration comes from simply hearing something beautiful or unusual; sometimes it comes from the wisdom of others or from kindness; sometimes it comes from nature. However, I am always inspired by people I know in my life who work hard and who have a deep knowledge of what they do—the ones who are real masters of their craft. I think it's important to learn from those people and ask for their advice and help when necessary. In general, though, I think inspiration is everywhere, every day, and it can be used in so many ways in your music.

SS: What would you say music did for/to you? Is there some part it taps into? Does it make you feel emotional? Could it ever be just a job?

RS: No, it could never be just a job, and I think sometimes it would be better if it wasn't. This is only because the business side of everything seems so all-consuming that I think it is swallowing the time people need to be creative and free, to just sit by a window and think and dream and feel something. So much can come out of that stillness—the constant movement and noise of social media and the pressure to promote takes so much away from everyone. Some of the happiest times in my life have been when I've been writing music and performing. They are two different feelings but equally as satisfying. There's a stillness in songwriting and an energy in performing that are both really fulfilling. If I'm feeling blue, a gig will always sort me out. And on a professional level, I think I've found a way to incorporate my drama training into my performing and feel satisfied with that, even though I don't get the chance to "act" as much as I used to, I am still acting, just through a different medium.

SS: What would you say to an aspiring female musician? Would you recommend music as a way to make a living? What characteristics do you need?

RS: Realize when you are being given an opportunity. Without wishing to sound patronizing, this can be so hard to recognize when you are young. Don't throw these opportunities away on something transitory—really look into the future and think about what might happen because of it. Practice the art of self-discipline. Not easy! It is a habit, and if you know it is your weak spot, go to battle with it and try to take control. In general, the harder you work, the more you will see for your efforts. Don't ever judge yourself against others, but do listen with a healthy, attentive ear. There may be styles and tones that you discover and try to experiment with—this is great. But don't ever try to be like anyone else or do the comparison thing—it is a total waste of energy. Be generous with your peers and colleagues. If someone is doing well, be happy for them and tell them so. Nothing will come of berating yourself that you are not in the same place or feeling resentful. Be glad for your friends' achievements and work hard for your own—your time will come.

SS: If you had to explain the one thing (or more) you found which makes music worthwhile, what would this be?
RS: One thing? That's hard! I think it is inexplicable. But there is nothing like knowing you have done a great gig with a bunch of wonderful musicians whom you both admire and count as friends. Sometimes, there is a golden nugget of a moment, when you are on stage, where you feel transported by the music and completely inside it—those are moments to cherish. Sitting down to write a song and finding something wonderful that you are pleased and excited by—that is also an amazing feeling. I've been to concerts as an audience member where the performance is so sublime that it makes you cry, and that too is worth everything.

SS: Do you think the pandemic changed music and how we access it? Or do you think music and how we access it changes over time in any case?
RS: I think, with technology, the way we access music will always evolve. I'm a bit of a technical dinosaur and have always felt as if I was born after my time, so the technological side of things feels very alien to me. During lockdown, there were lots of wonderful online events to enjoy and I think some amazing work took place. However, there is a huge pressure on musicians now to have new videos to share every five seconds, and it's time-consuming and distracting. I miss the old days when you rocked up to a concert, hoping to see a new band, wondering what they will sound like without having watched a thirty-second snapshot of what they do on YouTube. It's never the same as seeing an artist live, and I think we are forgetting that in this age of technology.

SS: Thinking of that young aspiring musician, do you think it is possible to make a decent living as a musician? How would you advise her to do this and what might her strengths need to be? Does she need to be a businessperson, to plan, and get a good manager? What makes the difference between

aspiring, struggling, and being a success?

RS: I don't know! Ha ha! I think it's certainly possible to make a decent living, but as the saying goes, "have something to fall back on." I've always had other strings to my bow, and I've been grateful for that. These days it seems that we have to be a great PR person, our own manager, a technological wizard, and that's alongside what should be the most important thing: being a great musician and honing your craft. I'd love to have been born a bit earlier and have been making music in the sixties and seventies, but that wasn't to be! So, I think the ability to play the game and be open to suggestions and input can be helpful, but without ever compromising your moral integrity or artistic path. I wish social media wasn't necessary, but unfortunately it seems to be, and we're in the thick of it now, so I guess we have to go with the flow. I think the word "success" is very interesting and means so many different things to different people. If success to a person means selling millions of CDs, being a household name, and touring the world, then I don't have the answer to how that happens, but there must be a certain amount of luck, downright tenacity, and, hopefully, incredible talent. And I guess it also depends on whether "struggling" means it's your only way to make a living and that's not happening, or whether nobody listens to your music or comes to your gigs. I think we are always or should be "aspiring" in some way to create, to be more practiced, and focused. I think I struggle with these terms because somewhere in the world there is an extraordinary musician whom no one has ever heard of; they are sitting in their room, writing beautiful music, enjoying their work, feeling fulfilled and content, and that can be a success too, can't it? Obviously, there's a tragedy to that too, because we all might be missing out on something astonishing. I would certainly feel incredibly sad if I couldn't share my music with people. But everyone feels differently. Surely, to lead a creative life, in whatever capacity, is the most important thing and to feel at peace with that. Anyway, enough philosophizing! From a practical point of view, if we have to be our own PR managers, tour managers, etc., then planning is essential. Write everything down you want to achieve and the steps you are going to take. Lists are helpful, or mind maps—pin them up! Think about friends and colleagues who may have contacts or ideas for you and make sure you thank them and do something for them in return! I would also say that dividing your focus in too many directions can be a problem—laser-like focus seems to be the key to the most prominent musicians in the world. And a manager is ideal but not easy to come by.

SS: How do you see the future for music? How do you see it for female musicians? Have you noticed any positive changes—or not?

RS: One thing I've noticed that's changing is there is more of an openness about being a mother in the music industry. And about time too. I hope that we are leaving behind the days where women were seen as a nuisance or somehow an inconvenience if they were mothers, less appealing, and that they would be too easily distracted and therefore could not be taken seriously. What a disgrace! Surely that must be changing now. A wonderful organization called Mamas in Music has been set up by industry professional Mary Leay to support women who are musicians and mothers. They are a worldwide community and platform for mums in the music industry who partner with other organizations to offer a variety of interesting projects. It's a nice place to discuss and be open about the challenges women face with regard to juggling motherhood and being a working musician. I want to be the best mother to my daughter in every single way. I sometimes feel like I am racing against the clock to get everything done before I pick her up from school, and I want to make sure that when she's with me, I am devoting all my time to her. In an ideal world, this would always work out. However, there are times when it just isn't possible and the guilt you feel can be overwhelming. However, I think it's also important for our children to see us working toward our dreams and passions, and if we can include them in that, then it can feel like a really exciting process for them too. My daughter, who is eight, often walks around singing my music, and there is no greater pleasure than to hear her doing that. She is now old enough to come to lunchtime gigs and really enjoys being involved and cheering me on. She's the most important thing to me in my life, so of course she is part of my musical journey.

EVIE ASIO

Photo Credit: Karolina Weilocha

"Rejection is not a possibility; it's an inevitability, so celebrate your wins and learn from your losses."

Evie Asio is a London-based musician who graduated with a BA in music and developed a unique sound over a series of experimental projects, including her 2015 EP Conclusion *and the* Songs From Home *series on YouTube. When she released her debut single "Beautiful Love" in 2019, she was named as "one to watch" by Premier Gospel. She has performed at the Women Do South festival in Clapham, The Spice of Life, Proud Camden and the O2 Academy, Islington, London. She is currently a rising star in music and gaining a lot of respect from fellow musicians. Her music draws on many influences and from many genres.*

SS: Can you tell me how you came to play music and how you found the instrument you specialize in? Do you play other instruments?

EA: I was always obsessed with music, and really got to hone that obsession at school. I was the kind of child who would dance along to my parents' albums and make up music videos in my head. I remember doing steel pans and choir in primary school, and I started piano lessons in secondary. Even still, singing has always felt like my number one. I can still remember the name and face of the person who came to my primary school to start a choir for the first time. Choirs and school productions kept me going for a long time, but I was dying to have a singing teacher. I finally got a singing teacher when I was fifteen, by getting a scholarship after performing as the lead in my school musical. That's when I decided that I wanted to go to a conservatoire (I had no idea what one was, I just knew they did music there). At this point, I was introduced to the concept of Saturday Music School and joined the Centre for Young Musicians at sixteen. I did my Grade 5 singing in the first year I was there, and my Grade 8 in the second year—without it, I might have never been able to study music at university.

Alongside my music education in school, I was also getting interested in music at church. I joined the music ministry as a vocalist first, then a keyboard player much later. If school helped me to understand music from a theoretical perspective, then church helped me to understand it from an aural perspective, and the feeling of it. I used the techniques I'd learned from leading worship and connected it to what I'd learned in the classroom. The two together have become the foundation for all that I know musically, and I have carried this duality throughout my career as a professional vocalist. After I left secondary school, I taught myself further piano skills for songwriting. I also have an acoustic guitar and a bass, which I know on a very basic level. I've also picked up a bit of ukulele. I enjoy having an understanding of a lot of instruments because it helps when it comes to writing and arranging.

SS: What genres do you play—how do they differ/make you feel? Do you have a favorite genre and why?

EA: I will sing almost anything—I love the challenge. In my days as a function band vocalist, no genre was off limits, which I loved. However, I have often been described as a jazz musician, which makes sense because so many of my skills as a writer and performer come from my learning in jazz spaces. When I play jazz, I feel like my most "serious musician" self, and that's because of the respect that I and so many have for the genre—so much graft goes into it. But the title I use for myself is an "alternative soul" artist, because I feel like that better reflects the music I create and the way I sing. My favorite thing to do is to tap into different genres that I love and combine them with chords, melodies, and basslines that I also love. I've experimented with folk, classical, gospel, and electronic, to name a few. This is where the "alternative" comes in—I have a soul voice, and I use soul instruments, but I love to constantly challenge my interpretation of what soul music can be. I wouldn't say I have a favorite genre, but I enjoy singing most when I can feel the meaning of the song in the chords and melody.

SS: As a female, have you ever felt treated differently as a musician than if you were male? If so, can you tell me how and whether you were able to do anything about this?

EA: I am grateful that I have not had some of the horrifying experiences that some of my other female friends have had in the music industry. I think as a female singer there are certain limitations that people can expect you to have, which often made me feel underestimated, and I enjoyed outdoing other people's expectations of my musical knowledge and ability to hold my own. Even so, I began to internalize some limitations early on in my career. I didn't see female producers, so I felt as if there was no way I could produce my own music. When it came to writing my album, I started the process thinking self-producing was not an option, but through time, the pandemic, learning, and trusting my instincts, I broke out of those mindsets. Now, the word "producer" is firmly a part of my identity and the way I see myself.

I wanted to talk a bit about being a Black female musician, as that adds another layer to things. I am so grateful for many more spaces and opportunities that support Black art and Black female art, because when I first started to perform and share music it felt like I was constantly hitting brick walls trying to find my tribe. There is definitely a certain mold that Black female artists are expected to follow, particularly in the UK. But now there are a lot more of us who are up and coming or making it who are visible—that's really encouraging.

SS: Have you ever come across bullying in your career as a musician?

EA: I wouldn't say that I've been bullied. People say to remain in the music industry you need to have a thick skin, which is true. We all face rejection, and some are harsher than others. But apart from the odd internet troll, I haven't experienced actual meanness. I have met a lot of lovely, genuine people in the rooms that I've been in.

SS: What experiences in music have made you grow as a musician? Were there events that happened which had a profound effect on you?

EA: Two experiences come to mind. The first was when I started to gig around London during my early twenties. I was very naïve and didn't know how difficult it would be—I didn't feel comfortable accompanying myself, I couldn't drive, and my keyboard was massive. Still, my friend and I would lug around this huge keyboard on the London underground to get to gigs. So, I took time to get a driving license and practiced keys until I could become a self-sufficient performer. At this time, I also accidentally fell into several pay-to-play gigs. It made me more resilient, but I lost a lot of money along the way. I realized the things that I needed to do to make performing more sustainable for myself. I learned how to stop saying yes to every opportunity that comes my way.

The second experience was the first five months of the pandemic, when I was in the middle of making my album, and suddenly I had no access to any studios or professional recording equipment. As far as the album was concerned, all I could do was plan and think. It was painful, to say the least. I tried to stay positive for as long as I could, distract myself with home musical projects and learning songs on the piano, but all in all, it was very depressing. During that time, I got angry, and I cried. The isolation also added to my feelings of being stuck and anxious. But without that time, I wouldn't be the musician I am. Before then, I was so concerned about time, and about getting things finished before it was too late. The fact that I began to officially release music in the later part of my twenties was a significant reason for this, as it made me wonder if people had written me off before I'd even started. I needed a reminder that I have to take my time if I am going to do my musical ideas justice. The time also helped me realize that I can make this happen! I learned to trust my musical mind, and the ideas that I had took me through the process. It all comes back to those internalized feelings of "I need a male to come and save me" in this industry. Of course, as musicians, we are not islands. But after the first wave of the pandemic, I grew a much stronger understanding of what I bring to the table.

SS: Who inspires you? Not just musicians perhaps, but anyone, and can you explain how they inspire you and why?

EA: I am very inspired by strong women. My mum inspires me, and my sister inspires me. They are the people that showed me that you can be strong, joyful, and authentically yourself. I am inspired by a lot of singer-songwriters.

Although Eva Cassidy did mainly covers, I class her in this category because she sings every song like she has rewritten it. I was thirteen when I discovered her music; she taught me about singing with emotion. I sang a song of hers in a school showcase and bawled my eyes out—the audience did too. Because of her, I bought my acoustic guitar (although I can barely play).

I could name so many other musicians, but two songwriters, Brooke Fraser and Corinne Bailey Rae, stand out to me as they inspired my writing style. I heard their songs and thought "This is the kind of music I want to put into the world, music that makes people feel." I loved the way that everything from the lyrics to the melody, to the chords, to the structure, unites to tell a story. It gave me a path of a successful musician to follow that wasn't necessarily mainstream.

SS: If you had to explain, what would you say music did for/to you? Is there some part of you it taps into? Does it make you feel emotional? Could it ever be just a job?
EA: I would say music gives me a voice. I am a person that does not always know exactly how to say how she is feeling. Music has allowed me to express the emotions I am afraid to share, and the thoughts I cannot speak. The connection part is hugely important for me. It taps into the part of me that longs to connect with others, the part of me that loves people. Having something to channel my energy into, from when I was a little girl until now, I think has steadied me as a person. For every difficult moment in my life, there is a song, released or unreleased, that has been written. Growing up, I felt like music was my only option for a career. I was good at other subjects, but nothing else interested me. Nothing else excited me. The fact that I get to work with the thing that I love most in the world means every day is a dream come true. Alongside creating music, I work in music education, which is another deep love of mine. I honestly don't think it's possible for me to do anything else.

SS: What would you say to an aspiring female musician? Would you recommend music as a way to make a living? What characteristics do you need?
EA: The first thing I would say is to keep going. Resilience and persistence are so necessary. There are things that didn't come to me the first time around because I wasn't ready for them, or my music was not where it needed to be for certain opportunities at that time. Some things were down to timing, some things were down to discrimination. Some things were because I wasn't in

front of the right audience. And you don't always get to find out the reason why. But if you have the opportunity to learn from your mistakes and go again, then growth always comes. Following that, you have to know what you want. Once you know what you want, you can begin to understand from other people how to get there. The last thing I would say is to build and maintain authentic connections where you can.

I am fortunate because I can do music in a full-time job that I love, while releasing and performing my own music, and if you can do what you love as a career in this life, I would say absolutely go for it. But every road has its challenges, and you have to consider what challenge is worth overcoming. Having a steady income means that I can afford to release musical projects and pay for rehearsal spaces. But it does also mean that certain things take longer. My challenge is that I have to balance these different areas of my life, but what helps is that I have a passion for both. It would be very different for me if my full-time job was not in music.

SS: If you had to explain the one thing (or more) you found which makes music worthwhile, what would this be?
EA: What makes music worthwhile for me is the emotional connection that it gives. I love honesty, openness, and human connection, and that is what I try to do in my songwriting. But I also love the fact that music can go beyond words and express all of these complex emotions and nuances that we are born to innately understand. Music is a safe space for me to express freely and creatively; when someone connects with not just what I said, but how I said it—it means so much to me. It makes me feel as if they have connected with a very personal part of me. So, I think that despite the ups and downs of making music, it will always be something that I am drawn to, and that feels like a necessity for me.

SS: Do you think the pandemic changed music and how we access it? Or do you think music and how we access it changes over time in any case?
EA: I absolutely do, but I think it's quite hard to fully understand the change as we are so close to it. I think the pandemic brought about a lot of exciting new "possibilities" for creatives and made a lot of independent artists positively rethink what they can do for themselves. Making music from home has made creating music accessible for so many people. I loved the influx of "pandemic songs"—people were just being real about their experience, and we connected

to those songs. That being said, I think it has also caused additional pressure for some, especially when you feel like you don't have the finances or the access to keep up with everyone else. There was a greater expectation for artists to entertain, particularly through social media and content creators—and I have such a love-hate relationship with social media. Sometimes I need to distance myself from it so I can remain emotionally heavy, but then I feel like I am not capitalizing on a tool that will help me grow a fanbase. Mental health for musicians was a lot to take in, and the loss of financial income from touring for many people was a lot. Music is always changing, and every day there is a new thing that changes the game. Right now, it's the effects of the pandemic and technology, but there will always be something else.

SS: Thinking of that young aspiring musician, do you think it is possible to make a decent living as a musician?
EA: Absolutely! I know many musicians who make a decent living as a musician (and some make just a living). The most important thing to understand is that there's more than one way to do it. However, you have to be clear about what path you want, and you have a plan about how you want to get there. The great thing about working as a musician is that it can be more than one thing. Especially as a DIY artist, you must have so many hats, from management to PR, to content creator, while keeping your musical creativity intact. It's important to get the right people around you, whether that's a manager or like-minded musicians and people in the industry who want to see you win. People should seek criticism in the right places and be willing to grow. Rejection is not a possibility, it's an inevitability, so celebrate your wins and learn from your losses. But what is successful all comes down to you. I would argue that you should set your parameters early so that you don't get caught up in comparing yourself to other people's success. For me, being successful is reaching people across the world with my music and having the financial capacity to make high-quality music, so that the stories within these songs can be told well. I have made so much progress on these goals in 2022, but I am aware that I have quite a way to go.

SS: How do you see the future for music? How do you see it for female musicians? Have you noticed any positive changes—or not?
EA: I think the future of music is bright, if there are musicians who are willing to be bold and honest with their art, which I think there always will

be. I think in the local spaces there are a lot of exciting platforms for female musicians—music nights, radio shows, and initiatives to spotlight talent. And people respond because the music is incredible, and the community is authentic. I think there is still a lot of pushback in mainstream spaces, especially behind the scenes. I think there are a lot of people who want to protect a system that makes money but isn't making decisions for artists in the long run. Hence why it's the music "business." So, for that reason, I don't know whether championing diversity and equity, talent, or nurturing artists, will ever be worth more than making money. The one thing I hope for is that artists will continue to take matters into their own hands and that they can work the game in a way that allows them to do what they love, as well as live a decent life, and sleep well at night.

TO CONCLUDE

The journeys of female musicians are as different and individual as the women themselves. Women have an ongoing presence in music. Today, they are being appreciated and respected—not least because society will not tolerate discrimination. As we evolve, fewer incidents of misogyny occur in most industries and, finally, we can say this is becoming true for the music industry—ongoing advocacy on pay scales aside. However, if you count up the male and female artists performing at music festivals, getting awards, touring, and leading ensembles and orchestras, male musicians still outweigh females by a hefty percentage.

Female musicians tell me about prejudice still to be found, yet they also tell me about changes they have noticed and subtle, affirming positives that are coming about. People want to see change, not least musicians everywhere, and we are making progress. There are business-minded curators, festival sponsors, venue managers, and musicians themselves who realize the canny thing today is to support females and men equally because this is the way to gain a diverse audience. The more diversity, the broader the appeal, the better the industry. I recently spoke to a music festival curator who told me that once they instigated a push to encourage female musicians to take part, their audience grew visibly, with families and single women attending events.

Increasingly, the arts are finding funding difficult—there is always somewhere money could be better spent apparently. So, it is up to us, the concert-going music appreciators, and the music industry itself, to make change happen and keep the incentive for change alive.

We see a range of experiences in the interviews in this book. Maggie Nicols and Charu Suri talk of abuse and how traumatic the attitude of men toward women can be. Nearly all of them talk about the drive music gives them and how they feel compelled to play and perform, and how they feel lifted by the music itself and the support of friends, family, and fellow musicians, as well as audience reactions.

Natasha Seale and Rachel Sutton speak about being mothers and family life. There are tales of bullying, misogyny, hope, failure, re-assessments, and re-engaging with music and audiences. The women talk profoundly about what music means to them, how they deal with the negatives and the positives, and most of all, how music is at the very heart of their professional lives and all that brings with it. Destiny Muhammad—previously a barber—describes how she can bring her experiences in that profession to music when dealing with people, and sometimes, her ruthless dismissal of those who treat her with disrespect.

One thing that shines clearly in these interviews is how the musicians respect themselves and other musicians. They value their craft, and not in an immodest way. They simply understand they are curators of sound, bringers of emotion, and how deeply people connect through music.

THE FOLLOWING MUSICIANS AND ORGANIZATIONS HAVE KINDLY HELPED SPONSOR THIS PUBLICATION

The Fabulous Red Diesel

The Fabulous Red Diesel is fronted by singer-songwriter Kat Lee-Ryan, a powerhouse of vocal creativity and lyrical originality. Fabulous Red Diesel is a band that can fit into any space where you are free to create in any way you feel. The band consists of Kat and drummer Wil-Lee-Ryan (Duke Boom) and two of their best friends, Beatrice Gullick (Miss Bea Have) and Simon Dobell (Rabbi Jaffa Delicious). Kat Lee-Ryan's unique delivery and lyrical style combined with the stellar quality of the band mean they fit no single genre. Performance is a musical circus, exploring genres, telling stories, a rollercoaster of emotions, laughter, and dance. Fun it is, but the music-making is serious. The Fabulous Red Diesel has recorded eight albums and are heavyweight performers and creators who never lose sight of their love for the audience, and the joy that can be shared by playing simply amazing music.

www.thefabulousreddiesel.com
open.spotify.com/artist/0hnu3Gtr7Br22o5Hw3Fw8C

Rachel Sutton

Rachel Sutton is a singer whose tone and sense of swing makes her an engaging interpreter of both classic jazz and more modern repertoire. Also a talented songwriter, her album *A Million Conversations* was called "a revelation" by Jazz Views and displays her ability to write both achingly tender and uplifting music. Her love of theater shines from the heart of every song and her flair for entertainment, natural stage presence and easy rapport with an audience is gaining her a loyal following. Born and raised in the Kent countryside, Rachel grew up listening to the romantic ballads of Cole Porter and George Gershwin, the soulful sounds of Stevie Wonder and Billy Joel and the haunting beauty of Joni Mitchell, Janis Ian, and Judy Collins. A theater student at Glamorgan University and the Welsh College of Music and Drama, she went on to play some of the leading roles in Shakespeare, touring the UK and Europe. Rachel's vocal abilities landed her roles in award-winning shows at the Edinburgh and New York Fringe, propelling her into a full-time singing career. Her role in *Lansky: The Mob's Money Man* at the Queen Elizabeth Hall, Southbank and Cadogan Hall received wide acclaim. She has performed sell-out gigs at top London jazz clubs, as well as venues and festivals across the UK.

www.rachelsuttonmusic.com
open.spotify.com/artist/3LfoUDjAkH4XTkSLIOTrES

Natasha Seale

Whether delivering a repertoire drawn from the delights of the American Songbook or introducing her own original music, artist Natasha Seale effortlessly breathes life into stories presented through song. Raised by the sea—her mother, a Welsh opera singer/pianist, and father, an actor, both teachers—Natasha was round the clock exposed to a musically diverse diet. Her love for Sarah Vaughan, Peggy Lee, Sounds of Blackness and fellow Hastonian Liane Carroll took her in a different direction, from singing in wine bars to the ski resorts of Colorado singing with a jazz quintet in the Rocky Mountains. Hailed by Bebop Spoken Here as a "Jazz Lady at Heart," Natasha is a master's graduate from Bath Spa and graduate of LIPA (Liverpool Institute for Performing Arts), and over the years has amassed an impressive list of credits, including leading lady in London's West End (*Les Misérables, Aspects of Love, Mamma Mia*) and Despina in Glyndebourne's Hip H'Opera *School 4 Lovers*. Seamlessly, Natasha stepped into the world of acoustic jazz and pop music with the release of her critically acclaimed, self-penned debut album *A Bigger Sky.* This collection of nine self-penned tunes—"Timeless torch songs," "luxurious jazz-pop": *The Musician*—was highlighted by Nigel Beaham Powell (BASCA, PRS) as "A musically accomplished body of work," while Chris Leon of Fresh On The Net exclaimed, "Natasha sings between the notes—what a voice!"

With a penchant for creating "engaging" one-woman shows, she can be found touring with her all-star band. Most recently with *A Life in Song:*

Rosemary Clooney and *Universal Ellington,* playing Pizza Express Jazz Club, Crazy Coqs, the 606 Club. The show followed her equally successful *Rosemary Clooney: A Life in Song* (Queens Theatre, Riverhouse Barn Arts), which saw Natasha fronting an all-star band in celebration of the life and music of the iconic vocalist.

www.natashaseale.com
natashaseale.bandcamp.com

Jazz Bites Radio

JazzBitesRadio.com streams the finest jazz in all its flavors across four channels 24/7/365 worldwide. Created to support new and unsigned talent in the jazz music industry alongside their more famous peers, Jazz Bites Radio sponsors jazz festivals, albums, and live recordings to help support and profile new talent, and always free of charge.

JazzBitesRadio.com—Everything Jazz, Uncut.
www.thejazzrepository.org

FURTHER INFORMATION

Musicians' Websites/Contacts

ellenrowe.com
www.lenistern.com
Chinamoses.com
www.aminafigarova.com
www.jamiebaum.com
maggienicolscreations.com
www.zoerahman.com
simonebaron.com
www.charusuri.com
www.saraserpa.com
www.ruthgoller.com
www.jellycleaver.com
destinymuhammad.net
www.emmasmithmusic.co.uk
www.collettecooper.com
emmarawicz.com
natashaseale.com
www.brigitteberaha.com
jeaniebarton.com
rachelsuttonmusic.com
www.evieasio.com

Further Links and Reading

www.womeninmusic.org
mutualmentorshipformusicians.org
F-list: thef-listmusic.uk
Baku Music Academy: musicacademy.edu.az/az
jazzednet.org
www.juilliard.edu
www.berklee.edu

A Few Helpful Explanations

ASCAP is the American Society of Composers, Authors, and Publishers.
BMI (Broadcast Music Inc.) advocates for musicians' rights.
Sitzprobe is a seated rehearsal of orchestra with the singers.

Other Books by This Author

Women In Jazz (8th House Publishing)
In Their Own Words (8th House Publishing)
All That's Jazz (Tomahawk Press)
Pause Play Repeat (Independent publishers)
The Wonder of Jazz (Independent publishers)

THANKS

This book could not have been created without the input, support, and thoughtfulness of the musicians who contributed their time and consideration. For their patience, their thoughts on the cover choices, and their understanding throughout, I want to thank every musician in this book.

I would also like to add my thanks to a few people who have contributed in other ways, from support, to comments on the layout and cover choices. They include Ivo Perelman, Anthea Redmond, Jacques Redmond, my forensic editor Richard Sheehan, typesetter Kate Coe and cover artist Ken Dawson.

Milton Keynes UK
Ingram Content Group UK Ltd.
UKHW020605130923
428587UK00008B/21